INSPIRATIONAL PREACHING

THE PREACHER'S TOOLBOX
COMMUNICATING GOD'S WORD WITH POWER

INSPIRATIONAL PREACHING

JOHN PIPER
GORDON MACDONALD
SCOTT CHAPMAN
BRYAN WILKERSON
HADDON ROBINSON
JEFFREY ARTHURS
JOHN ORTBERG
And more...

Craig Brian Larson, General Editor

HENDRICKSON
PUBLISHERS

Inspirational Preaching

© 2012 by Christianity Today International

Published by Hendrickson Publishers
an imprint of Hendrickson Publishing Group
Hendrickson Publishers, LLC
P. O. Box 3473
Peabody, Massachusetts 01961-3473
www.hendricksonpublishinggroup.com

ISBN 978-159856-859-2

Printed in the United States of America

Fourth Hendrickson Edition Printing — April 2020

THE HOLY BIBLE, NEW INTERNATIONAL VERSION®, NIV®. Copyright © 1973, 1978, 1984, 2011 by Biblica, Inc.™ Used by permission. All rights reserved worldwide. (Italics in quoted scriptures are authors' emphases.)

The Holy Bible, English Standard Version. Copyright © 2001 by Crossway Bibles, a division of Good News Publishers.

Scripture quotations taken from the New American Standard Bible®. Copyright © 1960, 1962, 1963, 1968, 1971, 1972, 1973, 1975, 1977, 1995 by The Lockman Foundation. Used by permission. (www.Lockman.org)

Holy Bible. New Living Translation. Copyright © 1996, 2004, 2007 by Tyndale House Foundation. Used by permission of Tyndale House Publishers, Inc., Carol Stream, Illinois 60188. All rights reserved.

Page 47: Poetic passage from a sermon preached by C. C. Lovelace on May 29, 1929, as heard by Zora Neale Hurston at Eau Gallie in Florida. *Negro,* edited by Nancy Cunard (London, Wishart & Company, 1934), 50–54.

Library of Congress Cataloging-in-Publication Data

Inspirational preaching.
    p. cm. — (The preacher's toolbox ; bk. 2)
    ISBN 978-1-59856-859-2 (alk. paper)
    1. Preaching. 2. Inspiration—Religious aspects—Christianity.
BV4221.I57 2012
251—dc23
                2011041048

TABLE OF CONTENTS

FOREWORD

"Wisdom is supreme; therefore get wisdom.
Though it cost all you have, get understanding."
(Proverbs 4:7)

That verse certainly applies to preaching. As editor of PreachingToday.com since 1999, I have listened to many sermons, and it is sobering to consider how many ways preaching can go wrong, from bad theology to bad interpretation of texts, from extremes on one side to extremes on the other, from being a people pleaser to being a people abuser, from confusing hearers to boring them. If there is any group of people in dire need of wisdom, it is preachers.

We find that wisdom in Scripture in large measure, of course. But while the Bible is our all-sufficient source book for what we preach, and for the theology of preaching and the character of the preacher, it is not a preaching manual. For much of what we need to know about preaching in our generation, in our geography, we need wisdom from one another.

We need the insights of those who have preached for fifty years, who have seen fads come and go, who have made mistakes themselves, and who can keep us from repeating them. We need the new perspective of young preachers who understand where the culture is going in ways that veteran preachers may not.

We need to hear from contemporary preachers who have read the wisdom of the church collected over hundreds of years on the subjects of preaching, pastoring, the care of the soul, theology, interpretation, sermon application, human nature, communication. We need to hear the wisdom of other "tribes" within the church, for each denomination or movement develops its own way of preaching, with its particular strengths and weaknesses.

In this book series, you will find a breadth of such wisdom. Since 1999, PreachingToday.com has published articles each month from outstanding practitioners on the essentials of preaching. This series of books with Hendrickson will draw from that bank vault of wisdom, bringing you timeless wisdom for contemporary preaching with the goal of equipping you for the most important work in the world, the proclamation of the glorious gospel of our Lord Jesus Christ.

And week by week, through the ups and downs, ins and outs of their lives, your congregation will be glad they have come to the house of the Lord to hear you preach. In your voice, your flock will hear the voice of the Chief Shepherd, the Overseer of their souls.

Let it be, O Lord, by your grace!

—Craig Brian Larson, editor of PreachingToday.com

INTRODUCTION

When I was a fumbling, insecure young seminarian, I often wondered if I would ever make it in the pastoral ministry. I had some raw promise, but on most days I felt like quitting seminary and going back to the business world.

Then I met Doc. His real name was Dr. C. Philip Hinerman, the senior pastor of Park Avenue United Methodist Church in Minneapolis. "Park" was one of the first churches in the United States to forge a deep unity across racial and socioeconomic lines. During my four years at Park, Doc befriended me, serving as my mentor, spiritual father, and preaching model. Doc had an irrepressible (and what I considered a naïve) belief that God would do great things through my life and my preaching. On numerous occasions, as Doc spotted me in the distance, he would sweep his arm in the air and proclaim, "Hail, Mathew Woodley, the great one!" At first I would look behind me to see if there was another Mathew Woodley on my tail. But there wasn't; Doc really did call me "the great one." Then I thought that he must be teasing me, but he meant it.

Doc brought the same spirit into his preaching. No matter where he started in the Bible, Doc would take all of us—saints and sinners, the saved and unsaved, blacks and whites, rich and poor—on a journey straight to the cross. I'll never forget the sermon he preached on the life of Ahithophel, the adviser to David's son Absalom who committed suicide after Absalom rejected his counsel (2 Sam. 17:1–23). It's a tragic and apparently hopeless story. But somehow as soon as Doc finished preaching on that obscure Old Testament antihero, people started streaming toward the front of the church to repent and trust Jesus. I should have stopped to analyze Doc's homiletical approach, but I was rushing to the altar to receive prayer for myself.

Doc inspired people. By the time he finished a sermon, we didn't *have* to follow Jesus; we *wanted* to follow Jesus. Every week Doc fanned the flames in our hearts, and every week sitting under Doc's preaching made us love Jesus with a little bit more intensity.

There's something special about the preachers who have inspired us. Like Doc, in one sense, they're utterly infectious. Of course in Doc's case, to borrow a phrase from C. S. Lewis, this is the "good infection." When we're around inspirational preachers, we catch something from them. We catch their passion for a specific biblical text or theme. We catch their love for God. We catch a spiritual reality in their lives—namely, that they know and feel the beauty of the gospel.

Of course we aren't just catching a feeling from these preachers. Somehow they combine deep passion with biblical exposition, so by the time they finish a sermon, our minds have been informed and our wills have been quickened. Perhaps in some small way, inspirational preachers give us a dose of what those first disciples said about our Lord on that dusty road to Emmaus: "Were not our hearts burning within us while he talked with us on the road and opened the Scriptures to us?" (Luke 24:32).

The short introductions I've written for each chapter explain how each author in this book possesses a Doc-like spirit. Ultimately the ability to inspire people through preaching flows from one thing: leading people into the presence of Christ. In this sense inspirational preachers don't belong to some elite group. You don't have to twist yourself into some mold of hyperenergetic, caffeine-charged, ultraextroverted superpreachers. As Gordon MacDonald shares in this book, "A soul-deep sermon can come from the lips of a simple, stammering, uneducated person, or from the heart and mind of a Rhodes scholar." This book provides hope for all kinds of preachers with all kinds of personality types.

So what does it take to become an inspirational preacher like Doc? First, this book often mentions the word *vision.* Everyone has a vision for life, something that captures that person and serves as a map for life. Thus, Skye Jethani urges us to ask, what vision has captured the imagination of our people? Inspirational preachers gently assault our incomplete visions and invite us into an alternative vision: life in and through Jesus Christ. That's what Doc did for me. Doc possessed a massive intellect and a quick wit, but he always gave us a clear and compelling vision of Christ—his glory, love, beauty, and power. In the first chapter of this book, John Piper urges us to do the same thing by making the supremacy of God the goal of our preaching.

People never outgrow this need to hear and see a compelling vision of Christ. As Bryan Wilkerson reminds us, life has a tendency to beat people down. "Like a hiker on a trail," Wilkerson writes, "after a while our eyes drift downward. We begin to look at the ground in front of us, and walking gets tedious and tiresome. Inspirational preaching gets people to lift their eyes and look farther down the trail, to enjoy the sights around them, and to think about where they're going."

You'll notice that throughout this book the authors will contrast *inspirational* preaching with *informational* preaching. They aren't opposed to providing clear content and how-to's; they just believe that inspiration must precede information. As John Ortberg says, it's about "changing people's interior maps" not just "changing their temporary behavior." In other words, good preaching should certainly instruct and exhort and challenge, but all of that flows from a transformed heart, a vision rooted in Christ.

Second, inspirational preaching creates and corrects *desire.* It gives people the "want-to" they need to follow Christ. By lifting up Christ and his kingdom, it woos people into a whole new set of desires. This represents classic Christian spiritual formation. Earlier followers of Jesus often said that desires aren't bad; they're merely disordered. They're unruly, like a bunch of wild six-year-olds who refuse to stand in line, pushing and shoving each other. In the same way, our desires, which are good, just need to learn to line up and behave.

Inspirational preaching taps into our hearts and gently expands our desire for the right things. At one point in the film *As Good as It Gets*, a neurotic and self-centered writer played by Jack Nicholson turns to a female friend and says, "You make me want to be a better man." That's exactly where this preaching leads: People who truly understand the gospel *want* to be better men and women. It arouses what Jesus called a "hunger and thirst for righteousness" (Matt. 5:6).

John Koessler reminds preachers that people won't hunger and thirst for goodness if we stand over them in condemnation. Instead, God arouses good desires only as we stand with and for our people. Yes, we can and should preach prophetically. By all means, speak the truth in love, as Paul tells us. But in the end, do your people know that you love them? Are you on their side? Are they certain that you're their advocate rather than their judge and critic?

Third, the authors in this book call for *integrity*. In other words, they remind preachers that they had better practice what they preach. There's nothing less inspiring than preachers who don't live what they say from the pulpit. To state it more positively, when the message is alive and growing within us, it inspires our people to do the same. Or as Jeffrey Arthurs simply states: "A reservoir can dispense only what it has taken in."

So inspiration begins by asking the Holy Spirit to examine my heart: Does the good news of Jesus still inspire me on a daily basis? Does my preaching text inspire me? Have I met Christ in this text? In this regard, Lee Eclov advises us to start our sermon preparation with a simple prayer: "Lord, give me eyes to see the wow in this passage." This isn't difficult: Ask the Holy Spirit to preach this passage—and the whole gospel—to your heart before you preach it to anyone else. If your heart has been stirred, God will use it to stir others' hearts as well.

Fourth, inspirational preaching is *emotional*. Since we're often wary of emotions, the authors in this book remind us that the world needs clear and deep instruction and exhortation. But good leaders and good preachers change lives on an emotional level too. This certainly isn't foreign to the Scriptures. The Bible is filled with emotions and emotional responses. Michael Quicke's insightful article on John 11 reminds us that "your text has feelings."

Feelings matter—in biblical texts, in our walk with Christ, in worship, and in nearly every dimension of life. For instance, imagine these three scenarios:

You're out in the woods, and a large, angry bear starts lumbering toward you.

You're in the park eating lunch, and suddenly a huge man slaps a little girl across the face.

You're at a baseball game, it's the bottom of the ninth, and you're down by three runs, when your team rips a grand slam to win the game.

What do you experience in all three situations? You'll *feel* something—fear, anger, and joy to be more precise. Even Jesus, the Second Adam, the perfect human being and the Son of God, felt deeply. So it's certainly appropriate to ask, what does God want his people to feel from this text? Then as we enter into the text, we can follow Jeffrey Arthurs's advice: "Let out what God has put into your heart." After all, if you can let out emotions at a sports event, you can certainly let them out when you're sharing the gospel.

Finally, all inspirational preaching also leads to *transformation* in Christ. In the end our revived feelings should always lead us to obey Jesus. Otherwise we might end up like those people condemned by Jesus who said (and I paraphrase here): "Lord, Lord, did we not hear wonderful inspirational sermons in your name? Did we not have our hearts feel deeply about great themes of the Bible?" but Jesus will respond, "Depart from me; for I never knew you" (see Matt. 7:21–23).

Christ-centered preaching always leads to a practical end result: It changes lives for Christ. Scott Chapman summarizes this well: "People don't just need to learn about God; they also need to experience God." People who truly experience Christ and his grace will start to obey him. Specifically, Gordon MacDonald claims that we'll start to see long-term changes in four key areas of discipleship: (1) reverencing the holiness of God, (2) living in repentance, (3) loving God with our whole heart, and (4) serving others in Christ's name.

Vision, desire, integrity, emotions, transformation—you'll find these themes sprinkled throughout this book. But the authors in this book will also remind us that inspirational preaching isn't easy. It doesn't happen automatically. In this regard every preacher could begin with this simple prayer from Mark Batterson's chapter: "God, I don't want to invest my time and energy saying things that people are just going to forget anyway. Help me say things in unforgettable ways!"

But that certainly doesn't imply that the pressure rests on the preacher's shoulders. After all, we can easily mistake our "inspiration" for a biochemical adrenaline jolt. Is the sermon successful because people felt pumped up or excited? How do you gauge sermonic success? Did the sermon hit the target? The short answer is this: We don't know when the sermon hit the target—only God does. And that's a work reserved for the Holy Spirit. So study with the intensity of a scholar, pray like a saint, write the message like an artist, deliver it like an orator, and then wait for the harvest like a farmer; but in the end, know this: Only the Holy Spirit can make dry bones live and fruit grow from the hard earth of a human heart. So add your little drops to the Spirit's mighty downpour of inspiration, and he will "do immeasurably more than all we ask or imagine, according to his power that is at work within us" (Eph. 3:20).

— Matt Woodley

THE SUPREMACY OF GOD IN PREACHING

John Piper

The veteran preacher John Piper sets the tone for this book with a clarion call for a God-centered approach to inspirational preaching. Piper has followed this God-exalting focus for more than thirty years of pastoral ministry. As he observes in this chapter, in many ways we live in a God-neglecting, God-belittling, and God-despising age. Taking God for granted or belittling God's glory causes us to grasp for the trivial trinkets of this world. According to Piper, this shallow, God-ignoring outlook on life can seep into our churches and even our preaching.

Fortunately, as preachers we don't just have to throw our hands up in despair. For Piper, honoring God starts before we step into the pulpit and preach. It begins as we stand in awe before God, savoring, loving, and treasuring the glory of God. As we delight in God, we also have an incredible opportunity to challenge the world's outlook and exalt God: It's called preaching. Week after week people hunger for a God-exalting vision for their lives. Piper challenges every preacher by asking, "If you don't lift up the glory of God and wean them off the breast of [this] God-neglecting [world], who's going to do it?" What a high and holy calling! As you read this book, may that question stir your soul and inspire your preaching.

One of the great advantages of remaining at the same church for seventeen years is that your personal mission statement and your church's mission statement become one. Our mission statement says: "We exist to spread a passion for the supremacy of God in all things for the joy of all peoples." My personal passion to make God supreme took a tremendous leap forward several years ago when I read an excerpt from a journal called *First Things*. The excerpt came from a specialist in general relativity theory named Charles Meisner, a man who shared Albert Einstein's attitude toward organized religion about fifty years ago.

Here's the quotation:

> I do see the design of the universe as essentially a religious question. That is, one should have some kind of respect and awe for the whole business. It's very magnificent and shouldn't be taken for granted. In fact, I believe that is why Einstein had so little use for organized religion, although he strikes me as a basically very religious man. He must have looked at what the preachers said about God and felt that they were blaspheming. He had seen much more majesty than they had ever imagined, and they were just not talking about the real thing. My guess is that he simply felt that religions he had run across did not have a proper respect for the Author of the universe.

Lessons from a scientist about God's supremacy

I was cut so deeply by this that I pledged to redouble my efforts so that no one would be able to say this about me. Likewise, I desire to cut preachers today so deeply that we all would want this never to be said of them. The quotation is still a fair statement concerning much preaching in the American pulpit. Though my sampling is limited, Einstein's concern is still valid.

The famous scientist said four things. First, preachers haven't seen as much of the majesty of God as he had, staring through a telescope or studying physics. Second, he said preachers just don't seem to be talking about the real thing. Third, he observed, there doesn't seem to be a proper respect for the Author of the universe. And fourth, he said preachers seem to be blaspheming.

The charge of blasphemy is meant to carry a wallop. Preachers claim to be talking about the eternal, infinite, unchanging Creator of the universe, but it doesn't feel like it. For those who are stunned by the indescribable magnitude of the universe, not to mention the infinitely greater Author of the universe, a steady diet of psychological, soothing, and practical how-to's seems inauthentic. It gives the impression that we preachers aren't talking about the real thing.

You may remember from high school physics that light travels about 5.87 trillion miles a year. The Milky Way galaxy, of which our solar system is a part, is about a hundred thousand light years across. That means our galaxy is about 587 thousand trillion miles in diameter. It is just one of a million such galaxies within optical range of our stronger telescopes.

In our galaxy there are about 100 billion stars. The sun is a modest-sized star with a temperature around the edges of 6,000 degrees centigrade. It travels at about 155 miles per second and therefore will make its first orbit around the galaxy in roughly two hundred thousand years.

Scientists are awed by these things. They instinctively conclude that if there is a personal God who spoke this into being and, who, as Hebrews 1:3 says, "upholds the universe by the word of his power," there ought to be a certain respect for and fear of such a God. The manifold greatness and glory of this God should be ever present in the life of his people. They should be stunned by the limitless things they could say about his magnificence.

Isaiah 40:25–26 concurs,

> "To whom then will you compare me?
>   that I should be like him?" says the Holy One.
> Lift up your eyes on high and see:
>   who created these [stars]?
> He who brings out their host by number,
>   calling them all by name,
> by the greatness of his might,
>   and because he is strong in power
>   not one is missing.

Einstein felt some of this, and his response was that preachers were not talking about the real thing. If the God of the Bible exists, then what's wrong with our preaching? Surely the theme, spirit, and atmosphere of our preaching should be the majesty and supremacy of God. Everything else we talk about should be brought into relationship to this passion of our preaching and our lives. This raises two great questions.

The focus and passion of all of our preaching

The first one is this: Why should the supremacy of God be the passion and theme of our preaching?

I was once asked by a preaching journal, "Why do you make so much of the supremacy of God being the theme of preaching?" I replied, "Because the supremacy of God is the theme of redemptive history. In fact, the supremacy of God is the theme of God." God is ultimately what's supreme to God. If God is supreme in his own affections, then God should be supreme in our sermon planning.

A few years ago I was preaching at my alma mater. As I stood and looked over two thousand students, the first words out of my mouth were, "The chief end of God is to glorify God and enjoy him forever." My friends in the balcony did a collective double take. They told me afterward, "We thought you misquoted the Westminster Catechism, which says, 'The chief end of man is to glorify God and enjoy him forever.'" But having listened to the entire message, they knew it was no mistake. I meant it with all my heart. I believe it's the main point of the Bible. The chief end of God is to glorify God and enjoy himself forever.

Jonathan Edwards is a hero of mine. He made this life-changing point of which I speak in his book called *Dissertation Concerning the End for Which God Created the World*. The thesis is as follows: "The great end of God's works which is so variously expressed in Scripture is indeed but one, and this one end is most properly and comprehensively called the glory of God."

Now let me read you one passage of Scripture so that you get the flavor of why I say God's supremacy is the main heartbeat of God, and therefore should be the main heartbeat of preaching about God. In Isaiah 48:9–11, God says,

> "For my name's sake I defer my anger,
> for the sake of my praise I restrain it for you,
> that I may not cut you off.
> Behold, I have refined you but not as silver;
> I have tried you in the furnace of affliction.

For my own sake, for my own sake, I do it,
    for how should my name be profaned?
    My glory I will not give to another."

I think those three verses are the most densely concentrated, God-centered verses in the Bible. On six occasions in this passage God declares that he acts either for "my name's sake" or for "my glory."

God's glory is his passion. He created the world to go public with his glory. He created human minds to understand his glory. He created human hearts to delight in his glory. All my theology is summed up in this statement: God is most glorified in us when we are most satisfied in him. This is the Good News, that God's quest to be glorified and your quest to be satisfied are not at odds. They are one in worship.

So why do we make God supreme in preaching? Because God is supreme in the heart of God, in redemptive history, in salvation, in the Bible, in missions, and in prayer.

The supremacy of God and our preaching

Now to the second great question: How then shall we preach?

The answer is highlighted in the most God-centered sermon in the Bible, found in Acts 13. Paul arrives at Antioch of Pisidia and goes into the synagogue. He's invited to address the people, so he preaches a survey of redemptive history. However, he does it in a manner that is foreign to us today.

I ask you, preachers: Do you preach like that? I ask you, lay people: Do you talk like that? When you talk about the world, do you say, "God did this," and, "God did that"; "God raised up this president," and, "God put this president down"? Do you say,

"God ordained this sinful strategy," or, "God cut that thing when its purposes were finished"? Do you talk like that? Do you make him supreme?

We live in an unbelievably naïve and superficial age—though that is the last way most people would describe it. A. W. Tozer, however, thought to describe it this way. Something is superficial when the treatment of it involves everything except the main things. As a scholar you can say much intelligently about a great many things. Yet if you leave out the main connections, you're treating them superficially.

Therefore I conclude that the communication media in America is superficial. I conclude that the educational enterprises in our universities are superficial. I conclude virtually all history books are superficial, virtually all public education is superficial, and virtually all editorial news commentary is superficial for one simple reason: the incredible, unimaginable disregard for God in it all.

God is the main reality in the universe, the sustaining power of everything that is. Therefore any time you treat anything without relation to God, you are being superficial. The fact that this sounds odd to us shows how infected American evangelicals are in this God-neglecting, God-belittling, and increasingly God-despising age.

Therefore, pastors, I plead with you to make him supreme in your preaching. I pray for my sons and my daughter: "O God, in all of their learning, I pray that they would see you. May they see you in geometry, history, philosophy, and English. May they see you as they work on their spelling." I can hear the cynics say, "Right, Christian spelling! Give me a break, Pastor John!" But that's the way a superficial, God-neglecting cynic responds to talk about God-centered spelling.

I remember the day when my nonacademic, dyslexic son said to me, "Why should I care about spelling the way everybody else spells?" I countered, "Well, you won't be able to communicate as well if you don't learn how to spell the way everybody else spells." "I don't care about communicating well," he replied. "Why should I care about communicating well?"

The blasphemous, standard, contemporary answer to this question is, "If you don't learn how to spell and communicate, you won't succeed in business and make as much money." What a godless answer.

Here's another answer, the one I gave my son. "Ben, you should care about communicating and learning how to spell because you were created in the image of God. And God's a great communicator. You should want to communicate because you've got something infinitely important to communicate. You've got God to communicate. You've got salvation to communicate. You've got Jesus to communicate. You can't be indifferent, Ben, to communication. God is love, and we scorn his love when we are indifferent about communicating good news to our neighbors, when they desperately need to hear these things. You need to care about communicating because language was God's idea from the beginning. 'In the beginning was the Word. The Word was with God.' It was God's idea. He is not a God of chaos and confusion. He's a God of beauty and order. He's not a God of anarchy, even spelling anarchy."

If you don't care about the supremacy of God in spelling, then you won't get my plea tonight. If we preachers don't lift up the supremacy of God week in and week out, showing a passion for it in all things, such as spelling, voting, sex, eating, and the stock market, who's going to do it? Apart from our God-exalting preaching, our people won't have anything that will consistently call them away from our God-belittling, God-neglecting, God-despising culture besides you. But one or two hours a week they'll listen to you. If you don't lift up the glory of God and try to wean them off the breast of God-neglecting America, who's going to do it?

Let's pray.

> Almighty God, our heart's desire is that you would be magnified in our pulpits, in our Sunday school classes, and in our living in such a way that we would awaken to your glory and supremacy, and so that others would see him who made the world and is redeeming the world through Jesus Christ. O Father, draw nearby your Spirit and seal these things to our hearts. Apply them in our churches and in our missionary movement, I pray in Jesus' name. Amen.

John Piper is pastor for preaching at Bethlehem Baptist Church in Minneapolis, radio speaker for *Desiring God,* and author of *Desiring God.*

THE BIGGEST IDEA IN PREACHING

Haddon Robinson

Sometimes we assume that the average Christian won't get excited about doctrine. So some preachers avoid doctrinal preaching and focus on "how-to sermons" loaded with nice advice on helpful, "real-life" topics.

But in this chapter, master preacher and preaching professor Haddon Robinson argues that the Bible isn't just "a sprawling book . . . for solving [our] problems." The Bible exalts God and weaves a beautiful story about a Savior who intervened to redeem us. As Robinson reminds us, the world doesn't need good advice; it needs the power, authority, and wisdom of God. Sharing that inspiring message with our people will lead us into doctrinal preaching. Every sermon has the opportunity to ask: What does this passage teach us about God?

For Robinson doctrinal preaching doesn't have to be dull and impractical. The twentieth-century British author Dorothy Sayers once wrote, "The Christian faith is the most exciting drama that ever staggered the imagination of man. . . . The people who [killed] Christ never . . . accused him of being a bore." Every preacher has the privilege of proclaiming the "exciting drama" focused on

*Christ. If we can connect the doctrine to everyday life (Robinson
calls it asking the "so what?" question), it won't bore anyone.
Instead, doctrinal preaching will offer life-changing inspiration to
ordinary people.*

In some ways, you could say all the ideas of the Bible make
up doctrine. Usually when we think of doctrine, we think of the
great affirmations in the Nicene Creed, the affirmations most
Christians agree to and embrace. Different churches have doctrines that distinguish them from others, but on a basic level
when you talk about the great doctrines of the Christian faith,
you're thinking of those expressed in the ancient creeds.

Someone once asked me if I agree with the following statement: Doctrines are the most important ideas from the most
important Book. I quickly agreed—although I would add that
when you talk about the "most important" ideas, that begs for
some definition. There are doctrines that most Christian groups
agree with, and I would say they are the outstanding ideas from
the Scriptures.

Everything flows from our ideas about God

One of the problems people have with doctrinal preaching
is that it is often done in an abstract way that doesn't seem to
impact life. But ultimately the most important things we embrace are ideas about God and God's relationship to us, and out
of those flow things that affect our lives.

So, to begin with, we have to realize that the big ideas
of Scripture actually do affect our lives. These big ideas will
definitely impact what I think God is about in the world. For
instance, if I believe the Bible is just a sprawling book of rem-

edies for solving practical problems, that will lead me down one specific way to live the Christian life. On the other hand, if I believe the Bible is a revelation of God and its main purpose is to reveal God to us, then that will lead me down an entirely different way to live the Christian life. Those are two different approaches, and I think the second has far more validity than the first.

Now, we need to ask this: If doctrines are the most important truths from the most important Book, and they affect everything we do, how should these ideas find their way into our preaching, practically speaking? In other words, how should someone who's committed to expository preaching preach doctrine?

Let me offer answers to those questions. First, when we preach doctrine, we are doing what I call a "subject exposition." If this is a great doctrine of the faith, then it appears in a number of places in the Bible. In order to preach this doctrine, I usually have an anchoring passage, but I also have to look at other passages in the Bible that speak to this doctrine. This is actually more difficult to do with validity than going through a biblical book one passage at a time. This approach requires that I take each of the passages I think refer to this doctrine and look at them in their context to be sure they are saying what they say— rather than what I want them to say.

Second, as you preach through a book of the Bible and come to a literary unit—or a pericope—you could say to yourself, *What do I know about God from this passage?* If you ask that question, you will find that the same basic truths about God emerge again and again. So as you're preaching through a book, it's helpful to take time to see the doctrines in which the biblical writer is basing his thought. Both of those are legitimate doctrinal approaches.

Getting the big picture of doctrine

Of course it's not always easy to branch out and get the wider biblical view on a specific doctrine. How do we do that effectively? It's no use chasing through the Bible and looking up ten references, all of which essentially say the same thing. Sometimes it would be far better to stay in one passage. Years ago Donald Barnhouse used to do that. He would preach through a book like Romans, and every so often he would stop and preach the doctrine that was behind this book. Jim Boice did the same thing. He felt two things: It helped his people see the doctrines and understand them, and it was a good thing to do for homiletical purposes, because it gave variety to his preaching.

As a personal example, a while ago, I was working in 1 Corinthians 8, where Paul is dealing with the question of food offered to idols. He is arguing that there are two ways of deciding whether or not you should eat the offerings. One is through the knowledge of doctrine, and the other is through love—not love for your brother, love for God.

So you look at that passage and say: "What do we learn about God in this passage?" Paul says: We know that there is only one God, and if there is one God, there can't be five or six or seven gods. So an idol is nothing, and offering food to an idol doesn't change the nature of the food. The idol is just stone or wood. In the course of that discussion, Paul talks about the fact that we have one Father who is the Creator of all things, and we have a Savior through whom all things are created. But it's clear in that passage that there is plurality in the Godhead, because he makes the major assertion that there is only one God.

Paul is saying that knowledge helps you in dealing with idols, but it would be helpful to stop here and say that this passage points to a fundamental doctrine of the Christian faith. It's pointing to the reality that there is a Trinity—Father, Son, and Holy Spirit. In the Corinthian letter, you have the Father, you have the Son, a chapter later you have the Holy Spirit, and it could be helpful to say: "Paul is dealing with a very practical problem. These Corinthians didn't know whether they could eat food that was offered to an idol. But he goes back to an understanding about God that helps him to answer this very practical problem. What was that understanding?" And then go from there. It would be helpful for Christians to realize that, while Paul is addressing some very down-to-earth questions, he does so based on the knowledge of God. So as you can see from this example, we need to be sure we understand what the Bible is teaching us about God.

Unraveling distortions and wrong approaches

Unfortunately many people have distortions or misconceptions about doctrinal preaching. First of all, in some churches the sermons may address doctrinal issues that arise out of that denomination's creed. So the pastor will take a doctrine and proclaim it. It doesn't necessarily mean that the pastor is going to go to the Bible to help his people understand it; it's sort of, "We believe our creed, not insofar as it's true to the Bible, but because we believe the creed is the expression of the Bible." I think you're better off approaching the sermon that way than trying to force it into the grid of a specific biblical text. That ends up sounding like something concocted by a group of theologians after spending time in a smoke-filled back room.

Second, in other churches doctrine gets preached in very abstract ways. It's often preached as though the main goal was to stick stale propositions up on a blackboard. "I believe that Jesus is the anthropic person"; what in the world does that mean? And if the preacher stays at that level, the fellow in the pew gets glassy eyed. A preacher must communicate better than that if he or she wants to establish the need for knowing doctrinal truth.

Third, on other occasions, people have preached the doctrine of their faith group or denomination, but it leaves the smell of gun smoke: "We believe this, but other Christians don't believe this (or other people who *profess to be* Christians don't believe this)." We're right; they're wrong. They preach doctrine in this way, because they have emphasized what I would call minor doctrines and have ignored the major affirmations that we all have about God.

Providing practical applications

If preachers want to make doctrinal preaching come alive, they need to have practical applications. For example, I think of the writings of someone like C. S. Lewis in *Mere Christianity*. Lewis tried to set out the basic doctrines of the Christian faith—mere Christianity, essential Christianity. He did this for listeners to the British Broadcasting Company. And his book is an effective example of how you take the great affirmations of the faith and teach them in such a way that listeners will get it. He is excellent at using analogies and raising the thoughtful questions that a listener might have.

Of course there are always the questions to ask after you're through with a sermon: So what? What difference does this make? It's better to start there, because you are trying to convince the audience that this is not just something incidental but something crucial.

Preaching the drama of doctrine

Without deep and practical doctrinal preaching, our sermons devolve into cute little moralisms about our faith: We should. We must. We ought. Or we end up saying something like, "Here are three ways by which we can improve your financial situation." I heard a sermon a while ago on how to deal with procrastination, and for his first point the preacher said, "Go get a Day-Timer." I knew the sermon was in trouble when I heard that. Now, honestly, I have no doubt that when people left that church, if they were procrastinators, they thought it was a helpful sermon. But it was simply something that a motivational speaker could have done.

If people are raised on cotton candy, they aren't going to grow as Christians. When Paul writes to his young associate Timothy, he says that "all Scripture is inspired by God," and that all Scripture is profitable for doctrine, for teaching, for putting the fundamental truths in front of people, and "for teaching, rebuking, correcting, training in righteousness" (2 Tim. 3:16). We have ignored that first affirmation—that the Bible is given to teach doctrine. It's not the only thing it does, but doctrine is first, and out of that there is reproof, correction, and then instruction in right living.

The theologian Kevin Vanhoozer has written a book called *The Drama of Doctrine*. That's an interesting title; most people have never thought about the drama of doctrine. As we dive into the reality of doctrine, we find an interesting pattern: All doctrines about God and the Bible are held in tension—and in that sense doctrine is drama, because drama deals with tension. God cannot exercise his holiness apart from his love. He can't exercise his grace apart from his omnipotence. Our Lord was full of grace and truth; that's an enormously difficult tension. I know people who are big on truth but can be very, very ungracious. There are other people who are big on grace and are willing to sacrifice truth so they can be gracious. But our Lord was full of grace and truth; there is a drama about God. There are some things we can affirm, but we can never speak completely about, because we can't put God into a box; we can't put him into a formula. But it does give us a glimpse of what it means to know God. When we're talking about the living God, these glimpses aren't just tired affirmations; they're also vibrant truths that will transform our lives and our communities.

So as we consider the glory of doctrine, we need to ask ourselves: Do I really believe that God gave the Bible merely for some practical advice on how to have a happy marriage, how to get along with people, or how to be healthy and wealthy? Do I believe it's merely a textbook on good behavior or on how to be moral? If I believe that, then I am going to go searching the Bible for practical truth, but what I'm really looking for is just good advice. We don't need good advice; the world's got better advice than it knows how to live up to. It needs God; it needs the power of God, the authority of God, the wisdom of God. Christians need sound doctrine, and it's out of that that we can live well, both eternally and temporally.

Haddon Robinson is Harold John Ockenga Distinguished Professor of Preaching at Gordon-Conwell Theological Seminary in South Hamilton, Massachusetts, and senior editor of PreachingToday.com. He also is radio teacher on *Discover the Word* and author of *Biblical Preaching*.

AUTHENTIC INSPIRATION

John Ortberg

In this chapter John Ortberg makes a simple point: If preaching doesn't inspire people, it's not really preaching. As Ortberg bluntly warns, "Inspire or get out of the game." On the one hand, that seems to dump a truckload of pressure on preachers. Some preachers might try to crank up the inspiration by adopting the personality of a famous preacher. But Ortberg doesn't want us to squeeze into someone else's preaching mold, because God can use a wide variety of personality types.

So how do we become truly inspiring preachers? First, all inspiring preachers have one thing in common: They've experienced what they're talking about. They preach from their lives, not just their sermon notes. Second, every inspiring preacher is filled with the Holy Spirit. As Ortberg says, "To be inspired means to be filled or touched by the Holy Spirit." Third, inspiring preaching doesn't just focus on the mind and will (what we want people to know and do); it also focuses on the heart and the emotions (what we want people to feel).

In the end Ortberg isn't piling more pressure on harried preachers. If we keep practicing the basics of the spiritual life—obeying God, walking in the Spirit, being aware of our spiritual gifts, humbly loving our people and then helping them think about and feel with Scripture—God's Spirit will make us the preachers we need to be.

Someone once asked the president of the country's largest speakers' bureau: "What's the most important characteristic a person needs to be an effective communicator?" I expected her to answer "articulation" or maybe "intelligence." To my surprise, she answered, "They have to have passion."

She explained that people with passion can overcome any other obstacle, such as a limited vocabulary or even a speech impediment. If they have an authentic passion, they tap into something contagious, something that feeds and inspires the human spirit. Conversely, if communicators don't have authentic passion, they may have great technique or phrasing, but their listeners will only tread water.

Preaching, of course, is much more than communication. It is a God-inspired act. But what is true for human communication in general is certainly true for preaching in particular: it has to inspire. If it doesn't do that, it's not really preaching.

The elements of inspirational preaching

An inspiring sermon doesn't have to be complex; in fact, usually it's not. But when you listen to it, you get a deep sense in your spirit that says, *Of course it must be so. Life must be this way.* Thus it becomes a part of the way we view life, altering the way we believe and live. So inspiring preaching aims at changing people's interior maps rather than just changing their temporary behavior.

Of course while true passion and conviction are at the heart of inspiring preaching, first and foremost the event of preaching relies upon the work of the Spirit. I think all of us have had the experience of feeling as though we are being touched or gripped or moved by something, some power or force outside ourselves. To be inspired means to be filled with or touched by the Spirit.

The thrill of the experience, however, is not under our control and can become misguided. When I experience a deep internal response, it's wrong to try to go back to the same story, the same message, or the same song and demand that I have the same response. Sometimes I think of an idea that makes my heart beat and brings a tear to my eye, and I can't wait to get up and teach it—only to find out it was just too much coffee.

Internal resonance is important. It's a gift when it comes. But it is never infallible, and it isn't something I ought to insist on. This is one of the reasons it's so important that preaching be done by people who have the spiritual gifts of teaching and preaching. The preacher needs to be receptive and discerning to the work of the Spirit in this area.

It's a hard word, but it would be worthwhile for those of us who preach and teach to think of ourselves with honest judgment. If we consistently find that people aren't returning, aren't being moved, aren't being inspired by God to change—repenting, making Christ the leader of their lives, reconciling marriages—we need to ask the hard question: Is this really the area where God has gifted and called me?

When you listen to inspiring preaching, you get a deep sense in your spirit, saying, *Of course it must be so. Life must be this way.*

The person behind inspirational preaching

People often ask me if it takes a certain kind of preacher to be inspirational. I always say, no. I'm always struck by the wide range of people that I find inspiring. There are preachers like Tony Campolo, people who possess enormous energy. On the other hand, I'm also inspired by preachers like Dallas Willard or John Stott, people who are calm and measured, and yet they can also say profound things that make your heart skip a beat.

Among inspiring preachers, there is an enormous range of diversity in temperament, style, background, and tradition. People with the gift of preaching and teaching, no matter their personality, don't have to worry, *can this inspire people?* God uses all kinds of temperaments and styles to move the heart. The common denominator of inspiring preaching is when the preachers are actually experiencing the dynamic they're preaching about. It emerges so deeply from who they are and from their experience with God that it becomes deeply moving to the people who hear them.

That means that as a preacher you don't have to try hard to manufacture an inspiring sermon. That's always dangerous, especially for the person doing it. If you're not good at it, everyone will see through the attempt, making it even more ineffective. It's even more dangerous, however, if you are good at it, because then you can ride that ability to manufacture artificial passion. There becomes an incongruence between who I am and what I'm saying; and there arises a danger of falseness and hiddenness.

Passion should not be forced. There are times when I feel dry or dull, and when I try to make something artificially seem more dramatic than it actually is, that's when I'm prone to exaggerate, become deceptive, or simply communicate inauthenticity to anyone who is discerning.

The doorway into inspirational preaching

There are certain themes in Scripture and certain aspects of redemption that will always evoke a greater response than others.

For instance, because of the way I'm wired as a pastor, if I'm preaching on God's love or forgiveness, there's going to be a bigger heart response than if I'm preaching on, say, the inspiration of Scripture or stewardship. It's tempting to just go back to those connecting themes over and over. We all have certain themes we have a particular passion for. But our goal must be to build congregations that are balanced, thoughtful, and understand the whole counsel of God. Sometimes that means messages are going to be more instructive or cognitive than they are emotive.

When I put a message together, I often ask three questions:

What do I want people to understand?
What do I want people to do?
What do I want people to feel?

Transformational, inspiring preaching should aim at the mind, the will, and the heart.

Preaching that fails to inspire often forgets to ask the third question: Without manipulating or forcing it, how do I want people to feel? Perhaps I want them to feel the love that God has for them. Or maybe I want them to feel the suffering of folks who have been poor or marginalized. Maybe I want them to feel the pain of two people who ought to be in a loving relationship but have remained unreconciled, their hearts growing hard and cold and distant. Uninspiring preaching often addresses only what people need to think, without asking them to do or feel.

I've also found it helpful to ask myself, "Why is it important to talk about what we're talking about today?" If I cannot answer that question, I'm probably talking about the wrong thing.

Preaching must involve much more than an abstract lecture about some theoretical ideas. We need to think about the people we talk to in a week: the single mom, an elderly man whose wife of forty-eight years just passed away, a kid who's leaving home for college. How will they hear this? What will it mean? How does it matter to their lives? It always helps to think about real people. If it matters to real people living real lives, and if it's a significant theme of Scripture, it has the potential to be inspiring.

John Ortberg is the senior pastor of Menlo Park Presbyterian Church in Menlo Park, California, a featured preacher for PreachingToday.com, and author of *The Me I Want to Be*.

HELPING PEOPLE THINK HIGHER

Bryan Wilkerson

Toward the end of J. R. R. Tolkien's classic adventure story The Hobbit, *Gandalf, the wise mentor, turns to Bilbo, the unlikely hero of the story, and exclaims, "Well done. . . . There is always more about you than anyone expects!" That's Bryan Wilkerson's approach to inspirational preaching: In Jesus Christ there's more good news than anyone expects.*

All week long the world batters people with bad news, stripping them of hope and dignity, cutting them down, and discouraging their hearts. But then the preacher steps up to declare: "On the authority of God's Word, there's more to God's love, power, holiness, and redeeming hope than you ever imagined. And in Christ there's also more to you than you ever imagined."

Preaching does that. It lifts people up. The Gospel is hard news: It exposes our sin and declares that we can't save ourselves. But ultimately our good and gracious God will lift us up. So preaching doesn't have to focus on the negative and the tragic; instead, it can truly inspire people. Inspirational preaching doesn't just dispense information or exhortations. More than anything, it taps into and then expands our God-given desire to want goodness.

Realizing the glory of inspirational preaching

Inspirational preaching is preaching that lifts people. It lifts people on a variety of levels. It lifts their understanding of themselves, of God, of the world, and of history. Most people's thoughts tend to drift downward. They get discouraged about life. They begin to doubt God. They question their own abilities. This downward drift—intellectually, emotionally, spiritually— needs to be uplifted. Paul says, "Set your minds on things above" (Col. 3:2). Inspirational preaching helps people think, believe, and live on a higher level.

Second, it also lifts their sight, their vision of what life could be, from what life actually is. Like a hiker on a trail, after a while our eyes drift downward. We begin to look at the ground in front of us, and walking gets tedious and tiresome. Inspirational preaching gets people to lift their eyes and look farther down the trail, to enjoy the sights around them, and to think about where they're going. Inspirational preaching lifts people's sight so they can see what could be up ahead.

Third, it lifts people's spirits. People tend to get beaten down by life, worn down, put down. Inspirational preaching helps people believe in God, believe in themselves, and see what could be, rather than what is. So *uplifting* is the best word to describe inspiration.

Unfortunately, as I listen to sermons, I don't hear very much preaching that's truly inspirational. A lot of preaching is informational, telling people things they need to know—and certainly we need to do that. Part of preaching is instructive. Of course a lot of preaching is also exhortational, urging people to do things they're supposed to do. They should witness, tithe, serve, or pray. Exhortational preaching is creating a sense of urgency around those things. That's also important; we need to exhort people. Finally, there's also confrontational preaching, where we're correcting some false understanding of doctrine or behavior. There are times to be corrective or prophetic, but too often we leave out the inspirational element.

Inspirational preaching encourages people to do things they already want to do. Deep down followers of Christ want to be generous. They want to share their faith. They want to be closer to God. While it's important at times to exhort them to do those things, inspirational preaching taps into the desire they already have and liberates it, giving them the permission to try new things in their relationship with God. It fills them with courage, which is what *encouraging* means.

Consider a specific example regarding a sermon about tithing. Sooner or later, every pastor has to preach on tithing. A certain amount of that is informational, especially today when some people don't know what tithing means. So explain it; give them the information they need. And then move on and exhort them: You need to tithe. Start tithing. The church needs you to tithe. And that's appropriate, but don't stop there. Encourage people. Inspire them to want to tithe. Tap into that desire they have to be generous and help them imagine what life could be like if they became tithers. We leave that element out too often.

On a more personal level, recently I was doing a message from Romans 8 on the work of the Spirit. The congregation needed some information: Who is the Holy Spirit? How does the Holy Spirit work in people's lives? There was also an element of exhortation, as I reminded the people we can't live the Christian life in our own strength: We need to rely on the Holy Spirit. But I didn't want to leave it at that—sending them out after instructing them and exhorting them. I wanted them to want to be filled with the Spirit.

So at the end of the sermon, I used a John Ortberg illustration. Ortberg uses a story about the difference between rowing a boat and sailing a boat. It's a story about canoeing in the wilderness and how tedious and tiresome it can be to paddle a canoe hour after hour. But when the wind picks up, you can grab a poncho, tie it to your paddles, make a sail, and go flying across the lake. I said, "You can paddle if you want to, but it's a lot more fun to sail." People walked out of the message wanting to sail, wanting to be filled with the Spirit, and for weeks people referred back to that illustration.

Many people often try to categorize preaching in terms of answering the questions *how, what,* or *why.* Inspirational preaching seems to transcend those questions in some way. It captures all of them and lifts them to a higher plane, to where the congregation not only has understanding and a sense of urgency, but also the want-to, and the belief that they can live differently than they do now. Life can be better than it is. They can be stronger Christians than they are. The church can be more vibrant than it is. Helping people trust God will definitely inspire them.

In this way the sermon becomes much more than a means to motivate people through an "information dump." I had a church member who was a motivational psychologist. He had done some research in the area of what motivates people in the workplace and contrasted extrinsic motivation with intrinsic motivation. Extrinsic motivation is rewarding people externally with a bonus, a pay raise, a vacation, or benefits. Many companies will motivate their people with those kinds of rewards. But research has found it's far more effective to tap into people's intrinsic motivations, their internal drive to want to be successful, to want to be competent, to want to belong. If you can tap into those intrinsic motivators, you don't need the external ones.

People who are intrinsically motivated work better, last longer, and have more fun. They're better teammates. This psychologist helped us create that environment in the church. In fact, he challenged me to never use the words *should, ought,* or *must* in a sermon. For a couple of years, as a personal discipline, I tried to never use those words, and it was difficult. But I soon found myself using different language, words of invitation: Why don't you? You get to do this. What would it be like? Imagine doing this. It became more invitational rather than exhortational.

Evaluating yourself: How inspirational are you?

If you want to evaluate how inspirational you are as a preacher, you could ask yourself a few analytical questions. To start with, ask yourself this question: How often do I use the words *should, ought,* or *must* in a sermon? Listen to yourself. Look over your manuscript. Chances are, you're using them more than you need to and more than what's effective.

Then you could ask yourself: How many of your illustrations end negatively? A sad story or a story with a bad ending is gripping. Consider the story about the guy who ends up lonely because he doesn't join a small group, or the story of the couple whose marriage deteriorates because they don't work at their marriage. Those stories certainly grab people's attention, but the stories are negative, and thus they don't inspire other people. Preachers will sometimes use those negative illustrations because we know we can get people, but I'm not sure we get them where they need to go. So how many of your illustrations end negatively?

For example, one weekend we celebrated the multicultural emphasis of our church. We had invited a speaker to come, a

nationally recognized figure in the area of multicultural ministry, and he preached what he called a prophetic message. And
it was a very prophetic message. I sat in the front row cheering
him on, saying, *That's it, brother. Let us have it. Tell us what we
need to hear.* But the people were disheartened by it. When I
asked them afterward why they had such a negative reaction, it
was because all the illustrations were negative—the many times
that the white suburban church had blown it. They were all true,
and we needed a kick in the pants. But the end result was that
the people ended up feeling guilty and disheartened, as if they'd
never ever get it right.

There needed to be some hope. The passage that preacher
used certainly provided a vision of what life could be like when
God's people lived in unity, but we didn't quite get there. As
a general rule of thumb, every negative illustration should be
balanced by a positive. The sermon should either be equal or
heavier on the positive side.

Next, think about content. Do you tend to preach more out
of the Epistles or the Gospels and the book of Acts? If you work
mainly out of the Epistles, chances are you're more exhortational
in your preaching. The narratives and Jesus' preaching tend to be
more inspirational. If you're in the Old Testament, do you tend
to work out of the Prophets, which will be exhortational, or out
of the narratives and Psalms, which can be inspirational? So our
content has something to do with it.

Another simple question is this: How do people feel when
they leave the service? Do they leave smiling? Do they leave feeling optimistic and hopeful? Or do they leave feeling sad or so-
bered? There are times they need to leave feeling convicted. But
over the long haul, how people walk out of the sanctuary is a
good indicator of whether they've been uplifted or not.

Growing as an inspirational preacher

First, be biblical. In other words, inspirational preaching shouldn't be lightweight. It shouldn't be a string of stories and platitudes and self-help happy talk. That gets thin and lacks power. There's plenty of uplifting material in the Scripture. There needs to be scriptural content. We're lifting people's understanding of themselves, of God, of the world, and of history. Be biblical.

Second, I'll say it again: Be positive. It's easier to be negative. Negativity does get attention. It engages people emotionally. If you've been preaching for any amount of time, you know what will cause a congregation to feel convicted or burdened or sympathetic with someone's plight. We know how to evoke those kinds of emotions, but we don't want to leave people there.

It's harder to be positive. It's harder to create a spirit of joy and expectancy. But we want to work hard at being positive.

For example, I was listening to a message on PreachingToday .com by Pastor Leith Anderson. He preached a message on how the church should influence a nation and its culture. Most of us, when we begin to preach about our nation and the role of the church, will quickly get negative—the decay of the culture, the inability of the church to address issues, the declining morality and distinctiveness of the Christian church. It's easy to get negative.

But Leith didn't do that. He brought a positive perspective. I was inspired. After listening to that message, I was ready to go out and do something, because it inspired me. Leith Anderson was working out of 1 Peter, and 1 Peter was written to a church that was persecuted, suffering, and scattered. Peter had reasons to be negative, but Peter said, "Live such good lives among the pagans that . . . they may see your good deeds and glorify God on the day he visits us" (1 Pet. 2:12). The tone in Peter's letter is positive, and Leith captured it.

Third, be passionate. Inspirational preaching has an element of emotion to it. We have to allow ourselves the freedom to be emotional, to laugh out loud, and to smile. If we're feeling genuinely choked up, we shouldn't be afraid of that, or afraid of having people feel choked up over a gripping story.

Probably the best example I can think of is John Maxwell. His enthusiasm is absolutely contagious. He's one of the most inspirational speakers I've ever heard. He carries you along by his sheer joy and enthusiasm for life, as well as the moments of brokenness he's felt in his life or experienced in others'. By the end of a Maxwell message, you've been engaged emotionally, and you're inspired.

Fourth, be hopeful. In other words, describe a preferable future for people. Help people imagine what their lives could be like. "Wouldn't it be great to go to work every day knowing you spent half an hour with God talking over your day and allowing him to speak to you through the Scripture?" That's very different from saying, "You'd better not go to work without having your devotions." Another example would be, "Think of how liberating it would be to be able to give away 10 percent of your income every year. Think of how free that would make you from the control of money in your life." Play out for people what their lives will look like when they begin to live this way, because people want to live that way. They don't need to be beaten into it.

Fifth, tell good stories. There's nothing like a story well told that engages people emotionally, helps them imagine what their lives could be like, and lifts their sights and understanding and hopes in the world. That could mean a personal story from your life or something you find somewhere about someone else. We did a series on getting people involved in service in the church, and we called it, Getting in the Game. There was plenty of information about the importance of service. There was plenty of exhortation: "We need you to serve." But I sensed we were lacking that inspirational element. Why should people want to do this? So we used a clip from the film *Rudy*, about the young man who was always told he was too small to play for the University of Notre Dame's football team. If you've seen the movie, you know it ends with Rudy's teammates carrying him off the field after Rudy gets in for the last few plays. There was no way I could create that with words, but that little film clip created that emotion. The people said, "I want to be in the game." That alone, without the teaching, without the exhortation, would have just been happy talk. But coupled with the content, it was effective.

When using inspirational illustrations, we need to be careful. We need to use accessible illustrations that the average person can identify with. For example, one illustration a lot of preachers have used (including me) is the story of Telemachus, the ancient saint who, by his martyrdom, brought an end to the gladiatorial contests. It is a stirring story of someone who stood up for what was right, even at the cost of his life. It has an inspirational element to it. But it was a long time ago and in a very different world. If that's our only story, the average person thinks, *This isn't Rome. I'm not a saint, and that doesn't relate to me.* A similar thing happens on a lesser scale when we use spiritual giants as illustrations. The average person puts people like that in a separate category, and the illustration, while powerful, is out of reach for the ordinary person.

There's an illustration I've heard about forgiveness. It's the story of a family whose child becomes ill, is treated by a doctor but is misdiagnosed, and the child dies. Some years later the couple's second child becomes sick in the very same way, and the same doctor asks if she can treat that child as well. The couple not only forgives the doctor, but also trusts her to treat their second child. It has a wonderful ending, and it is a powerful story, but it's almost out of reach for the average person. I wonder if some people sit there and say: *I could never do that. So I'll just never be able to forgive.* It doesn't mean you don't use an illustration like that, but if you do, make sure you use another one that brings it down to earth, close to home. Think of a person down the street, someone from the congregation that allows everyone to say, *Oh, she's like me. If she can do it, I can do it.*

That story about the person down the street might not be as powerful but it's personal. It illustrates biblical truth, and it resonates with ordinary people. In the end it's wonderful to preach in such a way that people walk out of the room believing life can be better, that they can be people of God who make a difference in the world. It's a rewarding way to minister God's Word to people.

Bryan Wilkerson is pastor of Grace Chapel in Lexington, Massachusetts, and a featured preacher of PreachingToday.com.

PREACHING THE WOW FACTOR

Lee Eclov

I'll never forget the first time I attended a professional football game with my dad. I still remember the first time I looked at a drop of swamp water in a microscope. And I'll never forget the first time I liked a girl—and she liked me back. There's only one word to describe these experiences: wow!

Life is filled with these inspirational wow moments. As we prepare to preach, Lee Eclov also wants us to find that same sense of "wow-ness" in every Bible passage. According to Eclov, every text contains twists or turns that surprise and even startle us. So our first task as a preacher is to start with a simple prayer: Lord, give me eyes to see and ears to hear the wow in this text. Once the Lord reveals it to you, let the wow of that passage permeate your sermon and your delivery.

It's not an easy task. We live in a world that's hungry for and suspicious of wow experiences. To paraphrase a quotation from C. S. Lewis, "Almost our whole education has been directed to silencing this shy, persistent, inner voice of [wow-ness]." But as preachers we are keepers of God's Word. So pray about it, watch for the wow in your text; then notice it, write it down, and share it with a weary, wow-waiting world.

Every text of Scripture is meant to wow us. It may be a wow akin to coming upon the Grand Canyon, or it may be more like the wow of a kiss after a long absence. It might be like your wow over an athlete's catch or more like your first impression of the Vietnam Memorial. But every text of Scripture—if we probe and ponder enough—has a wow factor.

Students of Scripture know what it is like to open what looks like a very oyster-ordinary passage only to find within an unexpected pearl of exquisite holy beauty. Even longtime students of the Bible will be surprised to find from time to time a promise or a picture in God's Word that is stunningly new. Other times it takes long hours of persistent study to begin to lay bare the ingenuity of divine logic in one paragraph or a theme running under the surface of Scripture like a vein of gold. Still other times it slowly dawns on us that this familiar text has a fresh application we'd never thought of before, like finding a new use for old medicine. But however the wow comes to us, that wonder must find its way into our sermons.

There is a wow in every text because, first of all, the Bible is always counterintuitive to the natural mind. Every week I think to myself, *I'd have never thought of this if God hadn't put it in this wonderful Book.* Furthermore, God regularly deals in wonders:

"No eye has seen,
      no ear has heard,
no mind has conceived
what God has prepared for those who love him"
—*but God has revealed it to us by his Spirit.*
(1 Cor. 2:9–10, italics added)

David had the wow factor in mind when he wrote in Psalm 9:1, "I will tell of all your wonders."

Identify the wow factor

As I study a text, I keep my eyes peeled for the wow in the text. Where will I pause in the logical development and take God's people for a break at a scenic overlook? Where will we get out of the car, stand with our mouths open, and snap some pictures before we move on to the application or the next paragraph of the text? How do I choose the overlooks? Try these questions:

- What in this text grabbed me as I studied? What stirred my heart and prompted my worship? Don't be too quick to settle on your wow; sometimes the most wonderful treasures are found only after a long journey of study and prayer, and some frustrating dead ends.

- Where are the feelings in the text? Recently when I was preaching from 1 Peter 1:19, the very expression, "the *precious* blood of Christ, a lamb without blemish or defect," seemed to require that I help us all *feel* how "precious" Christ's blood is. *Precious* is a word that has feelings. If they understood only the doctrine, but did not resonate with Peter's wonder, the text was not well served.

- Have I asked God in prayer what he most wants his people to **feel** from this text? Where would he insert a painting or poem, fireworks or a story? When a passage seems bland to me, I especially need to pray that God would give me eyes to see and ears to hear the wow. Remember: Part of application is making sure people *feel* what God intended them to feel through this passage.

Stirring up wow

The challenge is when overfamiliarity has leaked most of the wow out of a wonderful truth. That's why I dread Christmas sermons. It's hard to find the wow again. We may face the problem when we come to a text about worship, heaven, salvation, or the love of God. With a furtive look this way and that, we admit to ourselves that this great God-Word actually feels, well, kind of ho-hum. And we know that if it is ho-hum to us, we'll have a dickens of a time turning it into fireworks for our congregation.

Wow doesn't come easily to people. We are often spiritually autistic, seeing truth with dispassionate analysis. The preacher cannot be only a professor; the preacher must also be a poet, painter, and prophet, determined to stir hearts for God's sake. Besides the regular equipment of rhetoric (voice inflection, pauses, vigorous words, earnest sincerity, thoughtful development, and so on), I have found that these tools work for me:

- Lay open the text's divine logic. We know for certain that God's logic is always foolishness to the natural mind yet wonderfully sensible to the spiritual mind. When your text has a line of divine reasoning in it (as Paul so often uses), you might first set out the way the world reasons. (Wouldn't you think that dying is losing, that suffering is joyless, that God measures our lives by the rules we keep?) Then lay open the gospel logic right there in the text, how Gospel A + Gospel B = Gospel C. Be like the teacher who shows first graders that mixing blue and yellow paint makes green.

- Fill in the colors of Bible stories. It's easy for some of us to go overboard when we get our hands on a Bible story, but we need imagination sometimes to help people see the wow in a story. Zora Neale Hurston wrote of hearing an old-time African American preacher named C. C. Lovelace describe how Jesus stilled the storm:

And he arose
And de storm was in its pitch
And de lightning played on His raiments as He stood on the prow of the boat
And placed His foot upon the neck of the storm
And spoke to the howlin' winds
And de sea fell at His feet like a marble floor
And de thunders went back in their vault
Then he set down on the de rim of de ship
And took de hooks of his power
And lifted de billows in His lap
And rocked de winds to sleep on His arm
And said, "Peace be still."

I doubt I could ever come up with a description as beautiful as that, but when I read that, I realize I usually give up too quickly.

- Open wide the text's metaphors. The metaphors of Scripture often carry their own wow, but we have a scholar's tendency to dissect biblical metaphors with our Greek word studies, rather than simply letting them paint their thousand-word picture. A friend commented that biblical metaphors are like a silver bullet in a sermon, but we're more likely to take the bullet apart and show folks the casing, powder, and lead, rather than shoot it.

Recently I was preaching to preachers from Hebrews 12, where we're told that Christians come, not to Mt. Sinai's law, but to Mt. Zion's grace. The writer piles on descriptions, one being, *"You have come to God, the Judge of all."* Rather than explaining, I tried to paint a picture: Take God's people to stand quietly in the courtroom of the Almighty. Tell them of the drama there—of their relentless and eloquent Accuser and of his air-tight case against them. Tell them of the Judge's unbending justice, and of sin's certain death sentence. Then tell them of justification and the substitutionary atonement. Tell them of the Judge's genius in satisfying his own nearly impossible demands by doing the unimaginable—rendering sinners righteous without violating justice. And tell them that now they need not tremble before this Judge, nor cower before this bar, but they are to come *boldly* to his throne, where they will "receive mercy and find grace to help them in time of need" (Heb. 4:16).

- Tell the story of this truth's impact on you or someone else. You might begin, "I remember the first time this promise really hit me . . ." and you tell your story. One Sunday my text included Matthew 9:36, and I came across a story told by William Willimon when he was dean of the chapel at Duke University. He told about walking across the Duke campus one fall afternoon during the Oktoberfest celebration with hundreds of students, some of them barely clothed, many of them drunk, rock music blaring everywhere. His friend Stuart Henry turned to him and said, "Do you know what the ultimate proof of the divinity of Jesus is for me?" Willimon thought to himself, *That's a strange question, especially at this time and in this place.* And then he answered, "No. What is the ultimate proof of Jesus' divinity for you, Stuart?" Stuart said, "It's that statement from the Scriptures that reminds me of just how differently from you and me that Jesus views all this. The verse says, 'He looked upon the multitudes and had compassion.'" That story brought the wow to the text.

- Capture the wow in a well-turned phrase. Quotations are hard to pull off, but sometimes they make the wow sing. Recently, for example, in a sermon about suffering, I used this statement from an unknown author: "We can sometimes see more through a tear than through a telescope."

Sometimes I sense the need for a pithy line to capture the wow, but I can't find one anywhere. I remember well the day years ago when I was complaining about that dilemma to the Lord, and I think he said, "Write your own! Write your own 'quote.'" I realized that maybe I could wordsmith a phrase that would do, that perhaps I could say something with a wow in it. It doesn't happen often, and it usually takes time and work, but it can be done!

The wow in a sermon is not always the most important part of the message. That may be the application, the clear statement of a doctrine, or the convicting prod of a story. But finding the wow factor in every text assures that sermons will have biblically grounded pathos and that sermons won't be lifeless lectures.

Lee Eclov is pastor of the Village Church of Lincolnshire, in Lake Forest, Illinois, a consulting editor to *Leadership Journal*, and a regular contributor to PreachingToday.com.

SOUL-DEEP PREACHING

Gordon MacDonald

No preacher walks before his people, pours his heart out, and then expects nothing to happen. Of course we want people to change. We want God to move through our congregation. We want to experience the Spirit's anointing on our preaching.

Gordon MacDonald cautions us that this legitimate desire for change usually doesn't happen the way we expect. He calls us to practice "soul-deep preaching." It's the kind of preaching that cuts deep into the soul (of the preacher and the hearers) and produces long-term results, not just a flashy quick fix. According to MacDonald, soul-deep preaching is first and foremost "an act of God." Of course God can use a preacher's combination of scholarship and imagination, but in the end God brings the change in people's souls, not the preacher.

How do we know if our sermons are making a deep impact? For MacDonald, as we walk with people over the long haul, we can look for four visible signs of fruit: (1) a deep sense of God's holiness, (2) a growing experience of God's love, (3) a spirit of repentance, and (4) a desire to serve others. If you want your preaching to grow deep, ask God to deepen people in these four areas

"Wherever Paul traveled, revolutions broke out. Wherever I go, they serve tea." So said an Anglican bishop lamenting his perceived lack of impact upon people.

We all know what he's saying. Particularly in the area of preaching. You spend hours in preparation, both spiritual and scholastic. You seek stories and illustrations that ooze meaning and significance. You search your own life to make sure that you are as transparent as possible. Then, when the moment arrives, you preach your heart out. Words flow, thoughts build, stories produce laughter or reflective silence, decision time comes, and you expect . . . *Pentecost!*

Moments later the people file out with opaque comments such as, "Nice sermon, Pastor," or, "You gave me something to think about," or, "You were really 'on' today."

On the drive home, your nerves are raw. Indeed, it was a nice morning, but didn't anything happen? Like a revolution, for example? Or did we just serve our usual tea?

I've made that trip home countless times. I've entered the pulpit feeling that I possessed the spirit of a John Wesley and come out of the pulpit feeling like Cedric the Entertainer. It's a blue moment.

Preaching in the Bible seems, at first glance, always to have provoked powerful reactions. Ezra and the Levites, for instance, taught the Law to the people, and the crowd could not stop weeping. Imagine being John the Baptist when the crowds cried out, "What shall we do then?" Then there's Peter preaching on Pentecost, and the hearers are "cut to the heart." What happened when Paul preached at Philippi and "the Lord opened [Lydia's] heart to respond to Paul's message"? Impressive moments, which set a high expectation for any preacher.

Some speak of "anointed" or "Spirit-filled" preaching as they reflect on the origin of preaching power. On the other end of the transaction, where words are received by the listener, I would describe it as *soul-deep preaching*.

Soul-deep preaching is several steps beyond brain-deep preaching or feelings-deep preaching or guilt-deep preaching. The former provokes conviction, conversion, brave new actions. The latter, a momentary experience of good feelings or an intellectual appreciation of a solid point well made. But not much more.

An old cartoon features a preacher saying to another, "When you come right down to it, I'm just a collection of clichés, but I think I've managed to combine them in a rather exciting way." That's probably not said by a soul-deep preacher.

Soul-deep sermons reflect the description of the "word of God" in Hebrews 4:12: "It penetrates even to dividing soul and spirit, joints and marrow; it judges the thoughts and attitudes of the heart." You don't get any deeper than that.

It's important to observe that not all biblical preaching got to the soul, apparently. Take the words God spoke to Ezekiel:

> Your countrymen are talking together about you . . . saying to each other, "Come and hear the message that has come from the LORD." My people come to you, as they usually do, and sit before you to listen to your words, but they do not put them into practice. With their mouths they express devotion, but their hearts are greedy for unjust gain. Indeed, to them you are nothing more than one who sings love songs with a beautiful voice . . . for they hear your words but do not put them into practice. (Ezek. 33:30–32)

Sounds like a pretty resistant crowd to me, people beyond "convictability" (a word I think I've coined).

Those of us with the call of a preacher long to preach soul-deep sermons. We know of preaching moments where scads of people responded to Jesus Christ or opened their lives to God's love. And we want God to use us similarly.

Of course that kind of preaching—the soul-deep kind—does not necessarily invite the kind of praise that satisfies the ego. But it might instigate various kinds of revolutions. Change of heart, change of mind, change of attitude, change in relationships, change of behavior. It elicits worship, repentance, gratitude, submission. It might galvanize people to march together in new directions with a fresh sense of kingdom purpose.

Our role in the soul

When I reflect on soul-deep preaching as I've read about it, seen it happening, and—dare I say—experienced it (a few times), a few thoughts come to mind.

Let me start with the obvious: Soul-deep preaching is an act of God. It shouldn't (and probably couldn't anyway) be reduced to mechanics or techniques. "Stand up and say to them whatever I command you," God says to a young Jeremiah (1:17).

A soul-deep sermon can come from the lips of a simple, stammering, uneducated person, or from the heart and mind of a Rhodes scholar. God is not limited when vetting his messengers. Intellectually Paul was at the top of his class; Peter was a working man. But both were tops in the soul-deep preaching department. Go figure.

But the person does matter. We do not live in a day when a person can separate from the crowd and assume something like an actor's persona at pulpit time. We're talking about a believable person whose personal holiness and practical faith are clear to see in the nooks and crannies of real life.

Gerald Kennedy paraphrases a quote from Martin Luther: "When I preach in the Stadtkirche [the City Church of Wittenberg, Germany], I stoop down. I do not look up to the Doctors and the Masters of Arts, of whom there are about forty in my audience, but I look upon the crowd of young people, children, the servants, of whom there are several hundred. To them I preach. To them I adapt myself. They need it. If the Doctors don't care to hear that style of preaching, the door is open for them to leave."

I was twenty-seven years of age, a senior in seminary, when I was asked to preach in a Baptist church in St. Paul, Minnesota. A few moments before I was to go to the pulpit, the host pastor suddenly leaned over and whispered, "See those guys in the second and third rows? That's most of Bethel Seminary faculty."

I felt the inner regions of my abdominal area rearrange, for the folks in the second and third rows were a formidable, austere-looking bunch. *What in the world,* I asked myself, *could I conceivably say to such a group that would compel their attention?* Luther's words would have helped me then.

Then I heard what seemed a direct message from heaven: "Don't preach; just *talk* out of your heart to them about what you've been hearing me say. You're prepared; you're ready; just *talk* to them."

A moment later I stood up and talked, quietly, personally, and as sincerely as I knew how. I didn't pretend that I was anything more than a twenty-seven-year-old who had been gripped by what the Scripture had to say.

"Talk to them." I've been trying to do that ever since. No stain-glassed voice, no laundered vocabulary, no attempt to be much different than if we met in the Dunkin' Donuts line.

A. W. Tozer wrote fifty years ago:

There are preachers looked upon by their people as divine oracles, who wag their tongues all day in light, frivolous conversation. Then before entering the pulpit . . . [they] seek a last-minute reprieve in a brief prayer. Thereby they hope to put themselves into the position where the spirit of the prophet will descend upon them. It may be that by working themselves up to an emotional heat they may get by, may even congratulate themselves that they had liberty in preaching the Word.

But they deceive themselves. What they have been all day and all week is what they are when they open up the book to expound it to the congregation.

The Word made fresh

A soul-deep sermon has to do with one's insistence on taking scriptural truth and casting it in a twenty-first-century frame. A challenging but not impossible task. Scholarship and imagination work together here to cultivate the curiosity of the congregation so that they are willing to crawl into the text with the preacher and appreciate why and how it was written and what the author was trying to say as he responded to the impulse of the Holy Spirit.

Having done that, it's to work with the assumption that ancient truth is transcultural: It speaks to the present time. And what does it say? How will that truth translate into life on Tuesday or Thursday in the marketplace, in the home, at school? What difference will it make? What does life for the biblical person look like?

I have loved telling the story of a ferret named Bandit that our college-aged son brought home years ago. After some months we had to ask Bandit to leave (behavioral problems), but no one could tell us how to appropriately evict him. When I suggested to the pet store people that we simply let Bandit go in the New Hampshire forest, they were horrified.

"He can't defend himself or survive," they said. "He's trained to live in a cage."

We must beware of sermons that teach people to survive only in the protected cage of the church and among Christianized people. Soul-deep sermons take the powerful gospel and place it in the context of the streets of this world where life is tough and people need courage and wisdom.

Urgency (I think we prefer the word *passion* today) is an interesting word when it comes to the consideration of soul-deep preaching. It is used to describe a preacher who really believes that the eternal destiny of human beings is caught up in the issues a sermon might address. This is a scary thought. Truth be told? I don't get the feeling that most preachers really believe that eternal issues are in the balance when they preach.

Readying the crowd

You get the possibility of soul-deep sermons when congregations are prepared to listen at soul depth. An Augustine, a Luther, a Calvin, a Wesley, a Spurgeon, and a Graham were effective when their audiences were strangely ready. But here's an opposite case in point: Jesus "could not do any miracles there, except lay his hands on a few sick people and heal them. And he was amazed at their lack of faith" (Mark 6:5). So Mark writes of a preaching day in the life of Jesus that could be labeled (forgive me, Lord) a strikeout.

A *strange* readiness, I say. Because there are times when God—for reasons we cannot understand—cracks through the hardness of souls and sends a sermon deep within. People repent; people change; people become, well ... wonderful people. What readies a congregation? These moments are most often prefaced by large amounts of prayer.

A worshiper in a Welsh church (1859) writes of such a strange moment when people would have been satisfied with a routine meeting. The pastor, having read some Scripture, made

> a few passing remarks thereon, (and) an influence was felt by all present, which we had never experienced in the like manner before. There was a beauty, a loveliness about the Holy Word which we had never hitherto perceived. New light seemed to be thrown upon it. It electrified us, and caused us to weep for joy. The feeling became general. All present were under its influence. The hardest hearts were forced to succumb ... and then we sang, aye, sang with the spirit, and repeated the hymn again and again—we could not leave off. Every heart seemed inspired to continue, and the last two lines were sung for full a quarter of an hour.

Poof! The second Welsh revival was under way.

Results of soul-deep preaching

We must not load on to the idea too much, but certainly some of the following attributes must be among the distinctive marks of soul-deep preaching. A sense of the holiness and majesty of God might be one mark. This is a God with whom we must not trifle. He is to be respected and heard.

Then we might look for a sense of the deep, deep love of Jesus—a love that is virtually irresistible and which overcomes every barrier of the hardened soul. Jesus must be preached so that one cannot imagine living without a relationship with him.

Add to that the imperative of repentance. How could people leave a soul-deep sermon without being impressed with their unrighteousness and their need to make things right with God? Beyond that: the intent to change—a realization that this attitude or that conduct must be altered under the guidance and empowerment of the Holy Spirit.

One more result: The listener imagines a way to go out the door and make a difference in the name of Jesus. Serve people; introduce someone to Jesus; right a wrong; protect a vulnerable person. Categories like these.

I wonder if soul-deep preaching isn't also characterized by a persuasive close. Salespeople use the word *close* to describe the moment when they ask a customer for a sale. Crass words for a preacher, but there does have to be a defined closure to a sermon, a clear description of the kind of response the preacher believes God expects. It has to be spelled out so that no one can escape the challenge.

Joshua had a great closer: "Choose for yourselves this day whom you will serve. . . . But as for me and my household, we will serve the LORD" (Josh. 24:15). He got a good response.

There's a spectrum in closing. At one end is the immediate response—when a preacher ends the sermon with an invitation. I like to do this occasionally. But I always warn people ahead of time. At the beginning of the sermon I say, "You need to know that at the end of this sermon, I am going to give an invitation. It means that I'm going to invite you—if God is speaking into your life—to leave your seat, come to the front, and kneel and let someone pray for you. So as you listen to this sermon, keep in mind that I'm going to challenge every one of you to think through whether or not God is speaking and if you are one of those who should respond to my invitation."

I have never had such an invitation go without response. People so warned are people thinking with great seriousness. And they come, and often it becomes a milestone in their spiritual journey.

At the other end of the spectrum is an open-ended response, when you tie a truth to something people will experience during the coming week. Here the key is for provocative questions or ideas to linger in their minds.

Not long ago I preached a sermon on perseverance and quoted Yogi Berra, "It's not over until it's over," and then made some appropriate applications. A few weeks later a couple approached me with a family story.

"Our ten-year-old daughter," they said, "was in a soccer game this week, and they were losing by a goal in the last five minutes. She heard the opposing team's coach say to his girls, 'It's almost over, and you're going to win.'"

After the game—which ended in a tie—she told her parents, "I heard that coach say that the game was almost over, and I remembered when Pastor Mac said, 'It's not over until it's over.' So I decided to play harder." She went on to score the tying goal.

Maybe that's not exactly the best illustration for soul-deep sermons, but if a ten-year-old can make a direct application days later, then anything's possible.

Remember why you're there

George Fox, the founder of the Quakers, was a soul-deep preacher. When he reflected upon what made him a person like this, he simply answered, "I took men to Jesus Christ and left them there."

There was a time years ago when (I'm embarrassed to admit this) I grew a bit bored with preaching. While it was important to me to preach good sermons, I began to forget that there was a purpose behind it, that there were results to seek.

"I'm not sure that anyone's going to change because of what I say," I told my wife, Gail. "I need to remind myself to preach for change."

She heard me. And from that point forward, whenever I arose from my seat next to her to go to the pulpit, she would (and you would see her do it this next Sunday if you were with us) grab my arm as I stood up and say in a half whisper, "Be a man sent from God; preach for change!"

She makes sure I remember the purpose of our preaching.

Gordon MacDonald is editor at large for *Leadership Journal*. He teaches at Bethel Theological Seminary and Gordon-Conwell Theological Seminary, and is author of numerous books, including *Who Stole My Church?*

INSPIRED AND INSPIRING

Jeffrey Arthurs

Have you ever been talking to someone who suddenly comes alive about a certain topic? Let's say the conversation shifts to Brazilian soccer, or Mozart's symphonies, or the best enchiladas in Chicago, and suddenly your friend's face lights up. He starts talking faster and waving his hands wildly in the air. What just happened? You touched a passion point, a topic that stirs that person with fascination and interest. He will express emotions; he can't help it because he's inspired.

According to Jeffrey Arthurs, for some reason we're reticent about doing that in our preaching. We keep our feelings in check—even when we're describing the Giver of every good gift and the greatest news in the world. In this interview Arthurs urges, "Let out what God has put into your heart." Of course that starts as we allow the Bible to affect us first. As Arthurs puts it, "A reservoir can dispense only what it has taken in." But don't let it stop there: Think about your people too, Arthurs reminds us. What are their dreams, joys, hopes, fears, and passion points? How can your message stir their hearts?

Of course our "inspiration" doesn't push people to holiness; the Holy Spirit does. Arthurs calls it "the mysterious movement of the Holy

Spirit." So it's our job to pour out what God has poured into us, but ultimately only God can change hearts.

As a professor of preaching at Gordon-Conwell Seminary, you hear a lot of preaching. How much would you characterize as inspiring?

Recently I counted the number of sermons I listened to in a two-day span, and it was sixty-three. How many would I characterize as inspiring? The minority.

We prize biblical preaching. If a sermon flows from the truth of Scripture, how can it fail to appeal to the emotions, to inspire the hearer to action?

Because Scripture is not the only element in preaching. If it were, we would not need workshops and other resources on places like PreachingToday.com. We wouldn't need all the textbooks and conferences on preaching. We would just stand up and read the Bible—or we could just work through it verse by verse, and the job would be accomplished.

But the preacher is involved, and if the preacher has a spiritual defect or is hypocritical or in some way hindering the flow of that message, then it probably will not inspire. We all know Phillips Brooks's famous definition of preaching—truth through personality. So the preacher is an integral, inseparable part of the preaching equation. Brooks meant more by *personality* than a happy personality or an outgoing personality. He meant person-ness, humanness, through incarnated truth. So the preacher's heart must be stirred if the listeners' hearts are to be stirred.

Hugh Blair, a preacher and a rhetorician in the 1800s, said there is a contagion among the passions. The passions spread from the preacher to the listeners like a contagious disease.

Today in the field of oral interpretation we call it empathy; the listeners mirror or reflect the emotional state of the preacher. But the preacher is an important element.

Would you say then that the character of the preacher is one of the major roadblocks to inspirational preaching?

Yes, I would. The character of the preacher, if we take Brooks's definition broadly, the personality, the humanness, of the preacher sometimes hinders or quenches the Spirit.

As I said before, the listeners are a crucial component also. If they are disconnected from what is being said, if they're disobedient to what is being said, then that might quench an effective response also.

How can we avoid just bringing a truckload of information and biblical principles and then dumping it out on people?

That's my burden. That is my vision for preaching, that it would be deep ministry and not just saying words, not just going through motions, even if they're accurate words. So how can it be more? To start with, soak in the Scriptures. Immerse yourself in them. Bathe in them. Use all of the Bible study tools that you have. But then also use your imagination, pray through the text, internalize it. Some people recommend reading it out loud, taking the Scripture on a walk with you, working your way through it in meditation. A reservoir can dispense only what it has taken in, and it must be internalized if we're going to give it out.

We have to internalize it until we're passionate about it, until we believe it and it has affected us deeply. We are living that text at least vicariously. We are putting ourselves into that text, and the Lord has put it into us.

To avoid an "information dump" we also need to study the other side of the preaching equation, and that's the listeners. Don't just study the text; think about the people. Think about them, pray about them, imagine who you'll be speaking to, and love the people. Some preachers get out a pictorial directory of their church and look at the people and families, and they imagine what they're going through. *How will she hear this statement? How will he react to this illustration?*

Perhaps we could say one of the barriers to inspirational preaching is distance, both distance from the text and distance from your audience.

Right. The preacher sounds like a book. You're saying true things, accurate things, but it's not striking the flint of the human condition.

I also suggest self-disclosure and real-life examples. Demonstrate the relevance of that text as it has affected you, using real-life or hypothetical examples. For those who are concerned about revealing too much, I find most of us are too reticent to reveal how the Lord is dealing with us, rather than going to the other extreme.

There's an attitude, a theological perspective, that says, "I believe in the power of God's Word and the work of the Holy Spirit, and therefore I don't need to provide a stirring delivery; I just need to give the Word."

I've lived in a few different parts in the United States, currently in the northeast, and I face that stance with regularity. There is a proper fear behind that attitude. We properly fear phoniness and playacting and being cheesy. Good. But the suppression of emotion is also a kind of pretense. Listen to the fans of your favorite sports team (around me it's the Boston Red Sox), and you will hear emotions that are varied and sometimes explosive and sometimes bordering on lament or joy. In the pulpit, if we suppress what has been internalized, that's a form of pretense. I coach preachers to let it out. Let out what God has put into your heart. If it's too much, we'll pull back from that. But often it's not enough. Everything in a sermon ends up being bland and flat rather than full of life and engaging. As a general rule of thumb, we're usually projecting less than we think we are.

Some preachers may get to the point where they feel, I do need to be more inspiring or I need to express more passion, and they might go about it by raising their voices or gesturing more dramatically. What are some other things we can do?

At some point in the preparation period, get alone and ask the Holy Spirit to preach the message to you. If you've got a manuscript, go line by line asking, *Lord, what does this mean for me? Can I say this with integrity? Do I believe this?*

On the practical level I would also say, watch yourself on videotape, or record yourself and then listen to yourself preach the message. Also, remember that the inspiration of preaching is not entirely under our control. It's a confluence of the truth and the right truth for these people, of how the Lord has ministered to you and how the listeners are responding. Then there's the mysterious movement of the Holy Spirit. He moves like wind. We see the evidence, but his inspiration is not under our control.

Can we be good judges of whether we are inspiring in our preaching?

Yes and no. In some ways we can judge the level of inspiration. Experienced preachers know when they are connecting.

There's nonverbal feedback from the listeners, and then there's some verbal feedback afterward. People ask, "Will you pray with me?" or say, "I need to think about that some more."

On the other hand, we have to acknowledge that no one can look into a human heart. Many times we don't know what the Lord is doing. Sometimes we feel like we are uninspired and uninspirational, but the Lord is at work sanctifying his people.

Jeffrey Arthurs is dean of the chapel and professor of preaching and communication at Gordon-Conwell Theological Seminary in South Hamilton, Massachusetts, and author of *Preaching with Variety*.

FIGHTING FOR YOUR CONGREGATION'S IMAGINATION

Skye Jethani

A friend of mine recently underwent cataract surgery. He told me that before the surgery his vision was perpetually clouded by a thin milky haze. Everything in his sight—words on a page, his wife's face, his son's sporting events—were affected by the haze. Then the cataract surgery utterly transformed his vision of everything. Suddenly everything was clean and clear.

In the same way, according to Skye Jethani, inspirational preaching starts by changing our vision. People usually don't change when we merely give them new information or tell them to do more things for Jesus. In this chapter Jethani says, "Inspire people toward a certain kind of life." Preaching begins with a battle to capture the people's imaginations.

But Jethani will also warn that preaching isn't the only component of transforming people's hearts. Preaching can give us new eyes to start the journey, but it can't always walk with people each step along the journey. That doesn't minimize the importance of inspiring people by casting a vision for following Jesus. Jesus cast vision all the time. Every sermon provides a wonderful opportunity to perform vision surgery, clearing away the film of this world and offering people the beautiful alternative of life with Jesus.

I attended a secular university with a large Christian ministry that was action focused. It was about impact, outreach, and events. As I got into leadership, I had an interesting experience with a guy a couple of years older than I who had been a mentor of mine. I ran into him on campus when I was a junior, and he'd been graduated for a year or two. I had a conversation with him in which he broke down in tears and said his spiritual life had been in absolute ruin since he left college. He said his involvement in our campus group and the events and activities around him were what had buoyed his faith, but the moment he got out of school and didn't have that support structure, he had no deep, internal communion with God or a self-generating faith.

That was a big wake-up call for me. I realized I could easily get caught up in believing that all the pizzazz around me constituted my spiritual life, while failing to pay attention to the interior world. That was where the need for spiritual formation first hit me. That realization stuck with me through seminary and into the ministry, where it's so easy to get caught up in all the external elements that they become a substitute for an internal communion with Christ.

The goal of preaching: spiritual formation

This realization has impacted my preaching. My main goal on Sunday morning is no longer that people retain the information I'm presenting—that they would store it away in their brain as a reservoir of facts or truths or principles. My goal is now more toward inspiration. I want to inspire people toward a certain kind of life.

Of course this doesn't happen automatically. There are certain things that inspire people on the path of spiritual formation. For instance, stories are enormously inspiring; and not just biblical stories, but testimonies of people living or dead whose lives have been shaped in a way that reflects the life God is inviting us to. What does not tend to inspire people is giving them lots of concrete how-to's. Often I'll limit application to one thing, and I won't even make it a to-do. I'll just say, "Here's an idea," or, "Here's something that occurred to me when God was working on this issue in my life." That approach bothers some people because they've been taught you have to give concrete application so people know what to do. But I'm more concerned with whether they have caught a vision and whether they intend to apply it in their lives.

That's why preaching needs to be integrated with the whole ministry of the church community. If we're speaking about a particular issue over time, presenting a vision for what that looks like in God's kingdom, people have a variety of ways in which they can acknowledge their intention to follow through on the vision. It's not a cookie-cutter process.

The importance of vision

That's why an overarching vision is so crucial. Vision is imagining your life fully immersed in God's kingdom or imagining how Jesus would be living your life. For example, we preached a series last January about poverty. We tried to lift up God's character and his compassion for the poor and consider what our lives would look like if we had God's character regarding the poor.

We all have a vision that's driving us—and often one that has been given to us by the world. When you can identify what that is in your community, it becomes the enemy; it becomes what you are trying to deconstruct in people. Paul would write an epistle knowing what a certain community was up against, and he would present a vision that counteracted it. Most of his epistles are vision at the beginning, and then the latter part of the letter is where he gets to the meat. Children, submit to your parents; wives, husbands, slaves—all those application points come at the end. The vision is at the front.

What has captured people's imaginations in our contemporary setting is the vision of our consumer culture. That's what drives how most people live. So what we need to do is offer an alternative vision for their life, which means deconstructing what people have currently bought into. When it came to the issue of poverty and money, we highlighted the sinister nature of what most of us believe about money and identified where those notions come from in our culture. Then we lifted up the vision of what money looks like in God's kingdom.

My desire is not merely to give people what they want, but to transform what they want.

Until you have a vision, you can't choose it, which is what we call intention. Until you've chosen to follow the vision, you're not going to employ the means to actually get there. In other words, we put the cart before the horse in highly pragmatic preaching. So the vision of my life lived in God's kingdom is very important. Vision makes it possible to imagine life without lust, or to imagine being so generous that you would give away your most prized possessions, or to imagine living with such peace that you could handle the most traumatic events of life without losing your balance.

In one sense *vision* is another word for theology. It's what captures your imagination. Until that vision captures your imagination, you're not going to live that kind of life. You're going to live the life your culture calls you to live. When I preach on Sunday morning, I feel I'm battling the culture for the imaginations of these people. Of course the Holy Spirit is the one doing the battling, but my responsibility is to present a vision of life in God's kingdom that they're not getting anywhere else.

That's why stories are so important in casting a Christ-centered vision. The word *imagine* comes up a lot. It may include giving time for people to reflect or even stopping in the middle of a sermon to have people write down on a piece of paper what their lives would look like. I encourage people to come up with concrete ways of applying the vision to their lives, because I can't do that. I can give examples from my life, but I want them to think about the vision in their lives.

How to preach for spiritual formation

Here's what I'd recommend for pastors who have never thought about preaching for spiritual formation before. First, there's nothing wrong with pragmatics and giving people concrete application, but we often divorce preaching from the rest of the church and think everything has to happen from the pulpit. I think a much healthier approach would be to use pulpit ministry—and every other ministry of the church—for what it's best at. If I present vision from the pulpit, I want a means to fulfill that vision to come in somewhere, such as a small group or a support group. Pastors need to think through the role preaching plays in their church's whole ministry of spiritual formation. Don't isolate preaching from what's going on in the rest of the ministry. When we try to accomplish everything through the sermon, we often cram too much into it or focus on something it's not as effective at addressing. I don't think preaching is best at getting down to those concrete pieces of people's lives. It's much more effective at inspiring a vision.

Second, we pastors try to be too entertaining. We're really concerned about whether people like our preaching. That focus leads some pastors to take surveys in their church to find out what people want to hear about: marriage, kids, work, or finances. Then they present sermons that target those felt needs. That's not inherently wrong, but my desire is not merely to give people what they want but to transform what they want. If people have been primarily formed by the culture around us, what they want is probably not what they should want. Imagination and vision help people want what they didn't previously want. It's quite beautiful when John and Peter enter the temple, and the beggar's there asking for money. Peter says, "I don't have gold or silver, but what I do have I'll give to you. Stand up and walk, in the name of Jesus" (see Acts 3:6–7). He didn't give the guy what he wanted; he gave the guy what he needed.

As an example, let's compare a traditional homiletical approach to Philippians 4:19—"My God will supply all your needs according to his glorious riches in Christ Jesus"—with an approach emphasizing spiritual formation. The traditional approach would be to focus on God's promise to supply all our material needs. But the spiritual formation component in this passage is worry. We live in a society that keeps us scared about finances and security, so that we feel we always have to accumulate more. Jesus tells us not to worry about tomorrow; God will take care of it.

If I were preaching this passage, I would try to paint a picture of a life without worry. I would ask, "What would your life look like if you didn't worry?" That gets back to the character of

74

God himself, which is Jesus' point in the Sermon on the Mount: If God clothes the fields and takes care of the birds, surely he will take care of you too. The issue is our perception of God. If our imaginations are consumed with God's character, we're not going to worry, but if our imaginations are consumed with what the culture is telling us, we're going to worry constantly.

At the end of the sermon, I would invite people to think about applying the godly vision to their circumstances by deciding what spiritual disciplines might help them reject the worldly vision. What things trigger worry for you? If it's the news, stop watching it for a season. In other words, the application of that passage may have nothing to do with money. Instead, application may focus on answering the question, how do I deconstruct worry in my life?

We could contrast this approach to sermon preparation to an approach to preaching that looks for how-to's in the text. For example, let's consider the Epistles. The key is interpreting any part of an epistle in its context. When Paul lists concrete application ideas in the latter chapters of his letters, he alludes to the foundational theology he establishes at the beginning of the epistle. In 1 Corinthians 7, for example, Paul offers multiple applications about staying as you are: If you're single, don't get married. If you're uncircumcised, stay uncircumcised. If you're a slave, stay a slave. The principle he's teaching is that the external circumstances of your life are not ultimately important. They don't necessarily have a spiritual impact on who you are.

I know some people who are very committed to preaching verse by verse through a book, and that's a wonderful way to preach vision. But if you're going through an epistle verse by verse, you may spend months in the final chapters. In every sermon, you have to remind people of the vision the book is addressing. We can preach with a microscope and get so into the detail that we lose the vision, or we can preach metanarrative all the time and never offer application. Both extremes are problematic. But in our culture, which wants the pragmatic—give me three alliterated application points so I can go home—we tend to preach with a microscope. Our responsibility is to have the whole vision in mind, from metanarrative to the microscopic, and know at what altitude we are presenting each Sunday.

Sharpening the power of preaching in your church

We try to play to the strengths of each of the church's ministries. Preaching has its role. Relationships have their role. Serving has its role. Private disciplines have their roles. We've realized that if somebody comes to worship, attends a small group, and is serving somewhere, they're probably hearing between three and five different messages a week. That's overwhelming.

There are seasons when we make sure all our teaching is focused on one thing. We did that with a series about poverty. The preaching cast the vision. We presented the means to fulfilling that vision downstairs in one large adult class. We addressed the question: How do we apply this in our circumstances? This gave people concrete ways to apply the principles in their lives. The third component was small groups. Small groups were where people's intention was made clear. In small groups people cut to the chase and asked themselves: *Am I actually going to choose this? What are the obstacles in my life?* Vision, intention, and means were all focused on one area of spiritual growth, and we tried to fit the component of spiritual formation with the proper venue for that component.

Over the past couple of years, we've tried it at different seasons. At Advent, for example, we preach a vision of service—of giving ourselves away to others. We stop all of our classes and convert the church building into booths where families and small groups can do service projects that impact missionaries, people in our neighborhoods, and the poor.

We are always deciding where people are best able get the *vision,* where are they going to get the *means,* and where are they going to make their *intention* known.

Evangelistic preaching has operated this way for hundreds of years on a much more compact scale. The preacher gets up and presents a vision—either a vision of going to heaven or a vision of going to hell. Then he calls you to make your choice, and the means by which you make that choice is to raise your hand or say a prayer or come forward to the altar. This kind of preaching may have oversimplified the gospel, but it did get the three movements right: vision, intention, and means. We need to think this way about formative preaching as well.

Regarding intention, I like it to be a physical element in a worship service. If we're talking about money, then getting at their intention may mean providing an opportunity to give. I once preached on spiritual friendship and relationship. Then I invited people to talk to a spouse or friend about what they're going to do this week to connect more meaningfully with somebody with whom they want to grow in a relationship. So I'll give them an application idea or a point, but quite often it's difficult to get people to acknowledge intention in a worship service.

Another way to do it is to plan an event to reinforce intention. For example, if I preach a number of messages presenting a vision for a life without anger, I might offer a retreat the following month, during which we focus on the issue of anger and the disciplines for rooting it out of our lives. Their intention is expressed by signing up for the retreat, and the means will be presented at the retreat.

When you examine the Gospels, you find that most of Jesus' preaching was vision casting. So if we really want to preach like Jesus, we need to learn how to preach vision. That means we need a ministry that's structured to handle the means. We'll be limited in what we can accomplish as long as we depend on preaching alone.

Skye Jethani is a featured preacher on PreachingToday.com, a regular contributor to *Leadership Journal* and the author of *The Divine Commodity* and *With*. Jethani preaches regularly at Blanchard Alliance Church in Wheaton, Illinois.

PREACHING WITH VIM,
NOT JUST VIGOR

Bryan Wilkerson

There's a wise Jewish adage that says, "The heart is small but it embraces the world." No wonder Bryan Wilkerson, quoting Dallas Willard, contends that "we live from our heart." Real change starts in the heart.

In this chapter Wilkerson argues that God changes our hearts through a three-step process: vision, intention, and means (or VIM for short). In the previous chapter Skye Jethani paid particular attention to the first step in the process of heart transformation—vision. Now Wilkerson also helps us focus on the next two stages: intention and means. Intention involves a decision. Will I respond to the vision or not? Means involves the how-to, the plan, the steps involved in implementing the vision.

In the journey of following Jesus, this process takes time. It's tempting to view preaching as a quick-fix for people, but deep and lasting spiritual transformation requires what Wilkerson calls "incremental preaching"—a slow but steady approach to preaching God's Word over the long haul. Vision, intention, means (VIM)—it won't lead to changed hearts overnight, but remember and be inspired by this: Our God will always remain in the heart-renovating business.

I still remember my first sermon as a pastor. In a fit of homiletical hubris that every seminarian will recognize, I decided to impress my new congregation by unlocking the mysteries of the Minor Prophets. I began with a message from Hosea on the holiness of God. As I prepared that week, I became convinced that this could well be the most important sermon I would ever preach. If we were to grasp the holiness of God, it would surely transform our lives, and our church would never be the same. I preached that message with passion and expectancy. But when I looked out over the congregation the next Sunday, we were pretty much the same crowd we were the week before.

There isn't a preacher alive who isn't at once both energized and dismayed by the sermon's potential to effect change. Why aren't people more deeply transformed by their weekly encounters with God's Word? The deficiency can't be with the Scripture, obviously. And most of us, even on our worst days, manage to communicate biblical truth with a measure of clarity, relevance, and conviction. So why don't we see more real, lasting change?

In his book *Renovation of the Heart*, Dallas Willard unpacks the dynamics of personal transformation. He begins by informing us that "we live from our heart." The heart, according to Scripture, is the control center of human personality. It's the deep, inner place where the mind, emotions, and will intersect, where decisions are made. Our hearts have been malformed by our fallen world and need to be reformed by the Spirit of God. That renovation of the heart, according to Willard, follows a predictable pattern involving vision, intention, and means—or VIM for short.

In the *vision* phase, we come to believe that a particular change is both possible and preferable. But desire alone isn't enough to produce that change. If it were, we'd all be fit, punctual, and debt free! At some point we have to decide—*intend*—actually to get in shape, be on time, or live within our means. But now, having desired and decided to change, we need tools and practices—*means*—that will get us to that new place, like a diet-and-exercise plan or an alarm clock that works. Any attempt to effect change that ignores these three phases will fail to form, or transform, the heart.

A year of transformation

A few years ago we sensed the need to lead our congregation to a deeper understanding and experience of spiritual formation. In light of Willard's insights, and the depth of change we were seeking, we decided to devote an entire ministry year to the effort and to apply the vision-intention-means template to our preaching and program calendar.

1. Vision. We began in September with a vision series from the Beatitudes titled Change of Heart: Eight Qualities of Christlike Character. The series was designed to paint a portrait of the kind of people we were capable of becoming in Christ, a picture so compelling that people wouldn't just "get it"; they would "want it." Week by week we worked our way through the Beatitudes, offering a simple description of each quality, seeing how it was displayed in the life of Christ and imagining what it might look like in our lives.

For instance, we said that to be poor in spirit is to be desperate for God—to need him and know it. We discovered the many ways Jesus expressed and demonstrated his complete dependence on his heavenly Father. We began to envision how God filled and attractive our lives would become if we were to embrace such dependence and humility.

To increase the visionary impact of the series, each week we invited an artist in the congregation to paint a picture that captured the essence of that quality. We unveiled each picture at an appropriate moment in the message and then displayed them on the walls of the sanctuary during the series. By the end of the eight weeks, we wanted to be like the people in the paintings; we wanted to be like Christ.

2. Intention. But wanting it wasn't enough. We needed to lead the congregation to a decision; to declare their intention of becoming such a person. We followed up the vision-casting series with a "Commitment Sunday," unpacking the call to transformation in Romans 12:1–2. Toward the conclusion of the service, we provided people with a simple spiritual assessment tool. We provided some time to reflect on the eight qualities in the Beatitudes and to respond privately to whatever change they sensed God wanted to work in their lives that year. Following the service, we invited them to mark the moment by visiting one of several large paper hearts we had hung on the lobby walls and to put in writing their prayers for the year: "Lord, give me a heart that . . ." Those hearts hung there for a few weeks to remind us of our intention to become more like Christ in some specific area of life.

3. Means. After a break for Advent preaching, we picked up the theme of transformation in January. Having embraced a vision for becoming more like Christ and declaring our intention to do so with God's help, people needed to know the means by which they could experience real change. We launched an eight-week series on the spiritual disciplines titled Interior Redesign: Making Space for God. We allowed the popular home design shows to serve as a metaphor for reordering the interior of our lives. We taught people to create space in their souls by practicing simplicity, silence, solitude, and stillness, and then invited them to fill that space through prayer, Scripture, reflection, and God's Spirit.

To support the series, we created some "sacred spaces" in our facility, in which people could practice some of the disciplines we'd been studying. We also made available to our congregation customized Grace Chapel versions of Scripture Union's devotional guide *Encounter with God* to support their daily time with God.

By this time, a palpable change had come over our congregation, and many of us were experiencing a fresh work of God in our lives. We changed the pace a bit during the Lenten season but then picked up the transformation theme again in the spring with an Old Testament series titled David in Real Life: Cultivating a Heart for God. Our purpose in this series was to review and apply all that we'd learned by tracing the real-life journey of the man after God's own heart. We closed out the year in June with a "Celebration Sunday" that included transformation stories and a message on glorification from Romans 8, reminding ourselves that one day we will, in fact, be "conformed to the image of his Son" (8:29). As I listened to the stories and looked out over the congregation, it struck me that we were not the same crowd that had gathered back in September.

The preaching journey

That year was so formational for us that we have continued to apply the vision-intention-means template to our preaching and program calendar. In the fall we cast vision for whatever it is we sense God wanting to do in our congregation that year. At the conclusion of that series, we call people to response, inviting them to declare their intention to pursue that vision with God's help. In the winter months, we provide people with practical teaching, tools, and opportunities that will become the means by which they will be formed spiritually. In the spring, we focus on applying all that we've learned to the realities of everyday life, relationships, and mission. As we craft the preaching journey, we build in some supporting initiatives or opportunities to enhance the journey. Last year we focused on a theme titled One Another: Becoming the Body of Christ, and this year, Doing Good: Becoming the Hands and Feet of Jesus.

In his book *Strategic Preaching*, William Hull makes a strong case for a year-by-year approach to spiritual and congregational formation. He calls for "incremental preaching," believing that lasting change is more often the result of many sermons rather than a few. (Have you ever responded to a congregational problem or need by saying, "But I just preached on that!"?) He encourages preachers to view each sermon as part of a larger "concerted effort to guide the congregation in achieving its God-given destiny one year at a time."

Recently I was publicly interviewing a couple at the conclusion of a message. As the man spoke, he referred to "our year of transformation" as a pivotal season in his spiritual journey. When he mentioned the Change of Heart series in particular, there was an audible affirmation from the congregation, as if they all remembered it too, from three years ago! I was instantly glad we'd taken the better part of a year to go after a theme and grateful to be reminded that our congregation's destiny doesn't hang on one Sunday's sermon.

Bryan Wilkerson is pastor of Grace Chapel in Lexington, Massachusetts, and a featured preacher of PreachingToday.com.

YOUR TEXT HAS FEELINGS

Michael Quicke

Think about some of the best Bible stories beloved by people around the globe: Daniel in the lions' den, David and Goliath, Jonah's flight from God, Peter's denial of Christ, Jesus praying in the Garden of Gethsemane. What do they all have in common? Well, many things of course, but all of these stories make our hearts beat a little faster because they brim with feelings—suspense, fear, anger, sadness, relief, and joy.

Michael Quicke focuses on one Bible passage (Jesus raising Lazarus from the dead) and demonstrates the rich emotional life within a preaching text. Clearly all the characters in John 11—Jesus, Mary, Martha, the bystanders—express deep emotions. Quicke wants us to see that every passage has an "emotional hermeneutic." In other words, understanding and then preaching a passage implies understanding the context, language, geography, and the emotions embedded in the text.

Rather than produce self-absorption, Quicke argues that when we study all the aspects of a passage—including the text's emotions—it leads us deeper into the original passage. Then it also "moves us to worship; it moves us to love [Christ]; it moves us to a deeper commitment with a compassionate Lord."

Emotion can be used to manipulate audiences. As a result emotions—particularly in Caucasian and Asian cultures—are often considered the "bad boy" by-products of good preaching; they are the dangerous streets we must traverse to get to the goal of moving people to respond. The nature of the word e-*motion* makes this clear. Good preaching does move people; it is *supposed* to animate them. Ah, but that means we must play with those bad boys.

In the narrative, prophetic, and poetic genres particularly, it is clear God intends that there be an *emotional context* in Scripture. This emotional perspective should be the basis of inspirational preaching. I call this emotional hermeneutics. If the preacher understands these texts properly, preaching these narratives, prophecies, and poems *will* inspire and animate a response from the congregation. In fact, God gave these emotionally laden texts for that purpose.

Here I will use biblical narrative as an example. After establishing the significance of emotional context within a narrative, I will show how it can lead to powerful, inspiring, and motivating preaching.

The nature of biblical narrative

Narrative teaches by *showing* us the truth rather than by telling us the truth. It *shows* us how to live (and how not to) rather than telling us how to live. The emotional context of the passage draws in an audience, helping them to learn the lessons God seeks to teach them. We connect with Bible characters and their situations based on how we feel in similar situations. Paul says: "Now these things happened to them as an example, and they were written for our instruction" (1 Cor.

10:11). Our identification with the characters is crucial for these lessons to be clear.

Historically scriptural narratives have suffered from the demythologizing and excessive allegorization of some preachers. However, another way narratives suffer is through our ignoring the emotional context. Perhaps the fear is that the approach is too subjective to produce a valid interpretation.

The exact opposite is true. Empty a narrative of emotional context or natural human emotional responses and you create a stilted, artificial, and less valid sense of what the authors of Scripture intended to convey. In some cases it could even lead to errors in interpretation. By contrast, when we understand and accurately infuse a narrative with the correct emotional hermeneutics, we not only bring it alive, we also bring to light some details in the story that might otherwise be overlooked.

The emotional context of biblical narrative

If we ignore the emotional context while emphasizing the historical, cultural, and literary context, we can rob the characters of their humanity. We should not paint every character with the same emotional brush. Not everyone reacts or responds the same to the same circumstances. That is where a larger "emotional context" may come into play. In those narratives where the emotions of the characters are crucial to meaning, God gives us a context for understanding those emotions, usually a glimpse at their personality traits in other passages. There are reasons why we see King David as passionate, Peter as bold and impulsive, and Thomas as doubting. Knowledge of those emotional characteristics helps us when we interpret passages involving those characters.

We find an example of this in John 11 and the raising of Lazarus. We have an emotional context set up by the characters involved (except Lazarus), the situation (an illness where Jesus deliberately delays responding to a call to come, and the result is death), and the relationship of the characters with Jesus (he loves them). If we ignore these emotional contexts, we will be more likely to misinterpret the text, making an otherwise electrifying, motivating, and inspiring narrative less than God intended.

The emotional context of the characters, particularly Martha and Mary, is crucial to grasping the meaning of Jesus' differing responses to them. Luke gives us a context for understanding Martha's and Mary's emotional makeup.

> Now as they were traveling along, he entered a village; and a woman named Martha welcomed him into her home. She had a sister called Mary, who was seated at the Lord's feet, listening to his word. But Martha was distracted with all her preparations; and she came up to him and said, "Lord, do you not care that my sister has left me to do all the serving alone? Then tell her to help me." But the Lord answered and said to her, "Martha, Martha, you are worried and bothered about so many things; but only one thing is necessary, for Mary has chosen the good part, which shall not be taken away from her." (Luke 10:38–42)

This snapshot into the two women's lives tells us much. By the Lord's own words we know Martha is "worried and bothered" about many things. We are stunned by the level of anger or frustration it took for Martha to get into the Lord's face and accuse him of not caring about her or her situation, then order him to issue a command to her lazy sister.

The explosion of frustration unleashed on Jesus would not have happened in an instant but would have built itself through more subtle signals. The passage invites us to imagine vivid depictions of Martha, fretting in that part of their Judean home where food was prepared, banging food utensils together, shooting fiery looks at her sister. She would "communicate" her frustration before speaking. (One woman in my congregation uses the phrase *cupboard cussing* to refer to the slamming of cupboards in such a way as to express displeasure without saying a word.)

Mary, on the other hand, projects a completely different emotional makeup. She sits quietly at Jesus' feet, listening and learning along with the disciples. She is willing to ignore her sister's formidable efforts to "guilt" her into work (doubtless she is used to it). The historical-cultural context places these two single women in a culture that would view their singleness as a curse. They would have been in a position of needing to impress these young, single men in Jesus' band with their domestic prowess, perhaps inspiring a potential suitor. Martha knew that Mary's choice to sit worked against this.

Mary demonstrates an independence of thought and action that later explains her extravagant decision to pour on Jesus the spikenard ointment, probably her dowry, despite the way others might evaluate the action (John 12:1–8). This quieter, more reflective (yet strong) personality sets the emotional context for the person we see in the second half of the narrative concerning Lazarus.

The narrative makes clear the strong emotional connection Jesus shares with the family:

Now a certain man was sick, Lazarus of Bethany, the village of Mary and her sister Martha. It was the Mary who anointed the Lord with ointment, and wiped his feet with her hair, whose brother Lazarus was sick. So the sisters sent word to him, saying, "Lord, *behold, he whom you love is sick.*" But when Jesus heard this, he said, "This sickness is not to end in death, but for the glory of God, so that the Son of God may be glorified by it." Now *Jesus loved Martha and her sister and Lazarus.* (John 11:1–5, italics added)

The strength of that emotional connection sets the stage for the narrative tension generated by the next verse. "So when he heard that he was sick, *he then stayed two days longer in the place where he was*" (11:6, italics added).

This inexplicable delay, given the emotional setup of the Lord loving Lazarus and the two sisters, provides the explanation for the responses we see and hear when he finally arrives.

Jesus follows divine purposes in the delay, seeking to display God's glory with the power of the resurrection and, in Johannine fashion, to demonstrate in deed what he announces in word concerning himself (11:25–26). When he finally approaches Bethany, word reaches the grieving sisters, and John records what follows:

Martha therefore, when she heard that Jesus was coming, went to meet him, but Mary stayed in the house. Martha then said to Jesus, "Lord, if you had been here, my brother would not have died. Even now I know that whatever you ask of God, God will give you."

Jesus said to her, "Your brother will rise again."

Martha said to him, "I know that he will rise again in the resurrection on the last day." (11:20–24)

The emotional context for this exchange is implied by the differing responses of the women to the knowledge of Jesus' approach, confirmed by the Luke 10 passage. Martha, assertive and vocal, has demonstrated she is unafraid to confront him if she is upset. Thus she goes out "to meet him." We can picture her walking, or perhaps better, stalking with the fierceness of an angry woman, her eyes blazing with hurt and anger.

Given Martha's prior confrontation in Luke 10 where *entitlement to help* was clearly an issue ("Lord, do you not care that my sister has left me to do all the serving alone? Then tell her to help me"), the interpreter should realize that entitlement would likely be on Martha's mind once again. She would feel deeply hurt by the fact that she had shown hospitality—fixed numerous meals, arranged bedding, and so on—not just for Jesus but for his entire entourage. Until Lazarus' illness, she had asked for nothing in return that the text records. Now she asks Jesus to do just one thing for her, and he does not come. This would seem to her extremely unfair, maybe even unjust, especially if he purports to love her.

Therefore she meets and confronts him with "Lord, if you had been here, my brother would not have died." Given the emotional context, this was not said in a mild way. She probably had her index finger out pointing in his face and spoke through clenched teeth. The emotional context and her own emotion draws us into the narrative. We *feel* it with her and resonate with and reflect on all the times we felt God was unfair to us.

The next verse is interesting and provides what I would term a hermeneutical watershed in the passage. She goes on to say: "Even now I know that whatever you ask of God, God will give you" (11:22). Numerous interpreters see this as an affirmation of her faith in expectation that he could help the situation even now. This makes little sense at an emotional level. She certainly has no expectation of Jesus raising Lazarus at this point, for her answer in 11:24 shows she thinks of the resurrection in "last day" terms, and she hesitates later when Jesus asks that the stone over the tomb be moved (11:39).

Interpreters sensitive to the emotional context should ask, what would an intense, angry person *say* in such a situation? She would probably explain *why* she is angry at him, why she feels the *right* to be angry at him. Likely, she is saying: "Even now I know God answers your prayers, and that if you had just been here and prayed for my brother, he would be alive today—but you *weren't* here, were you?"

Jesus' reply to this confrontation ("Your brother will rise again") anticipates what he is about to do, but the interpreter cannot assume Martha has knowledge of that possibility. It is wrong to read the end of the story back into the tension building in the narrative. Interpreters have to think again about how a woman who is hurt, angry, and confused by what outwardly appears to be callousness and neglect would respond to such a statement.

The nature of the relationship between Martha and Jesus and the emotional context of her grief and disappointment with him helps the interpreter understand her answer. She says, "I know that he will rise again in the resurrection on the last day" (11:24). This is her rabbi whom she loves, who has just said to her what religious leaders tend to say to grieving people. She hears one of the platitudes said beside caskets, similar to "he is in a better place now" or "you will see him again someday."

However, bitterness and disappointment are laced through her comment. Her "last day" strongly contrasts with the "even now" of 11:22. In other words, this platitude does not change the fact that Jesus did not come when she called, and now she has to wait until the last day to see her brother again. It is consistent within the emotional context to hear her saying, "I know he will rise again in the last day, *but a lot of good that does us now* since you did not show up!"

Inspiration in emotional release

If I am preaching the story of Mary, Martha, and Lazarus from John 11 (as I have at funerals and in other contexts), the resonance of the audience is usually palpable and the tension extremely high at this moment (11:22–24). It screams for release. We identify with Martha getting in God's face, index finger extended, expressing for all of us what we may never have the courage to say.

What answer could he possibly give her? Narrative tension is strong in every great story; it is what makes them great. It moves the audience to the edge of their seats. The roar of a home crowd is loudest when the winning touchdown is scored with seconds left. The greater tension produces the stronger release of emotion. People are ready to be inspired by this text, and I, as a preacher, should not disappoint them. God intended it to have this effect and to move people to faith and action.

Emotional hermeneutics are crucial here. As this devastated woman expresses her pain in fierce anger, Jesus does not run for cover. Her anger does not make her unsafe to him, and he does not distance himself from her. Nor does he slap her down for impertinence, dominate her, or crush her to wrest control of the situation from her and "put her in her place." Rather, at the emotional level, he meets her eye to eye, strength for strength, and speaks the truth to her heart. And what truth! To borrow from a TV channel promotion, "God *knows* drama."

More than giving Martha a platitude about the resurrection, Jesus confronts her with himself. She is mistaken to believe the resurrection is some *event* far off in the future. The resurrection is a *person*. Indeed, she is *looking* at the resurrection right here, right now. "Jesus said to her, *'I am* the resurrection and the life; he who believes in me will live even if he dies, and everyone who lives and believes in me will never die. *Do you believe this?'"* (11:25–26, italics added).

Jesus matches her assertiveness with his own—not over her, not under her, but *with* her—speaking truth into her grief. Confronting her with who he is in this situation, he asks her to believe. The narrative tension broken by the revelation is raised again by the question. That question echoes across the centuries to audiences today. Those seated by the graveside of a loved one are being asked the same thing. *Do you believe this?*

Martha, lovingly but clearly confronted with the truth of who he is, affirms her faith in him. "She said to him, 'Yes, Lord; I have believed that you are the Christ, the Son of God, even he who comes into the world'" (11:27).

Proving the importance of the emotional hermeneutic

That is not the end of the story. Mary, with her very different personality, has not yet confronted him. Martha goes and calls her (11:28–29). When she arrives, her response is very different from Martha's, but *her words are exactly the same!* "Therefore, when Mary came where Jesus was, she saw him, and fell at his feet, saying to him, *'Lord, if you had been here, my brother would not have died'"* (11:32, italics added).

The significance of the exact same words being used cannot be overlooked. How can we interpret a text word for word the same and say that something completely different is meant?

The only thing that makes the words different is the way they are said, their *emotional context*. The text itself cannot give us that, nor can the literary, historical, or cultural context, only the emotional context. Mary is not angry with Jesus, but she is no less disappointed. She chooses to express her broken heart at his feet, weeping. We know she is weeping by the next verse where Jesus sees her and others weeping. What we fail to understand, if we get the emotional hermeneutic wrong, is the significance of Jesus' response. "When Jesus therefore saw her weeping, and the Jews who came with her also weeping, he was deeply moved in spirit and was troubled, and said, 'Where have you laid him?' They said to him, 'Lord, come and see.' Jesus wept" (11:33–35).

Why would Jesus weep at this moment? The response seemingly makes little sense, and commentators are all over the map to understand it. Most think it has to do with the unbelief surrounding him. Why weep when you are about to rectify the situation? The crowd of observers also debates the meaning of Jesus' tears. So the Jews were saying, "'See how He loved him!' But some of them said, 'Could not this man, who opened the eyes of the blind man, have kept this man also from dying?'" (11:36–37). They do not understand the significance of the whole narrative, because they are not privy to it as we are.

So why *does* Jesus weep? Emotional hermeneutics gives us the answer. Because, as he demonstrated wonderfully with Martha, the Good Shepherd of John 10 *stays with* his sheep, whom he loves, when they go through the valley of the shadow of death. As Jesus stayed with Martha, not over her or beneath her, so now the Good Shepherd joins Mary where she is emotionally, weeping. He does this, even though he knows he will raise Lazarus in a few minutes. Jesus lives in the moment of grief with her and *shares* it.

This truth from the narrative is simple, profound, and inspiring. It moves us to worship; it moves us to love him; it moves us to a deeper commitment with a compassionate Lord who would come and share such moments with his people. Raising Lazarus becomes a miraculous sign of the truth of who Jesus is, but this narrative interaction between Jesus and the two sisters, and its potent emotional content, leads us to a far deeper, more personal place to identify with the characters and be inspired.

Michael Quicke is professor of preaching at Northern Baptist Seminary in Lombard, Illinois, and author of *360-Degree Preaching*.

ALLOWING EMOTION TO
BUTTRESS TRUTH

Gary Fenton

Whether we like it or not, our listeners are evaluating not just our sermons; they're evaluating us. And they're asking questions like: Does the preacher really believe this stuff? Does this preacher really care about people like me? Do the preacher's words reso-nate with his or her heart? These questions flow from a central concern: trust.

Gary Fenton isn't advocating that we "eliminate facts from our preaching." Obviously people still want to know if we've done our homework on the text. But especially in our age people are asking for "emotional credibility." Without denigrating deep and clear thinking, Fenton urges us to feel deeply about the Scripture, God, and people. In the past, we could get by with emotionally disengaged preaching and perhaps earn people's trust. But today if we want our listeners to trust us, we had better speak clearly and feel deeply. There's no other way to build trust so people can say, "Okay, you have emotional credibility, now tell me more about this Jesus."

I grew up in the 50s and 60s, in what some call the "*Weekly Reader* generation." *My Weekly Reader* was a little black-and-white newspaper distributed in grade schools that kept students informed on current events. Conventional wisdom of the 50s told us that facts were going to form the future, so the magazine was filled with facts. As a generation, we tended to trust facts and mistrusted emotion, and that affected our religious views as well. Emotional religion was for the uneducated, and religious teaching focused on the factual proofs for Christianity.

I learned that as a preacher I needed to prove factually that biblical principles "worked." If the Bible commanded us to honor our father and our mother so our days on earth would be long, I validated that injunction with statistics showing that people with happy families lived longer. While feelings could be manipulated, facts were the sixteen-penny nails of our faith.

Gaining emotional credibility

Things have changed, though. The generations behind me tend to trust feelings over facts. Their young men and women know facts can be manipulated, that there can be information without knowledge. Madison Avenue knows this well. Think of the Nike commercials on TV: They don't tell you anything about the product or the price. Nor do they compare Nike shoes with any other athletic shoe. They touch your emotions, showing an amazing athlete hanging above the rim while you hear the roar of the crowd. And that communicates to you that Nike makes a great shoe.

The use of emotion through image has serious implications for preachers. In a sense the ability of a preacher to evoke emotion in others—not in a manipulative way, of course—can help gain credibility and drive home the truth of the gospel.

I know a pastor who sometimes weeps during his sermons, and it's been fascinating to hear the different reactions of people in his congregation. One woman, embarrassed by it, said, "My pastor cries during his messages. Do you think maybe he's having an emotional problem?" On the other hand, I've heard younger people say, "That guy's authentic. He's got the real stuff."

My point here, of course, is not to imply we should use emotion irresponsibly or ignore reason. I'm simply trying to buttress my thesis that on a large scale, the way people think has shifted in recent years, and a pastor needs to continue to grow to be effective. Nor am I saying we eliminate facts from our preaching. Rather, we may want to use emotion strategically in our communication to increase our effectiveness.

Connecting early with your listeners

In 1998, for example, the Birmingham, Alabama, area lost thirty-four people in a tornado during Holy Week. A thousand homes were destroyed and hundreds of people were injured. On Sunday morning, the paper ran photos of all thirty-four victims on the front page. The paper included stories about each of the victims. The tragedy was on people's minds as they came to church, and I needed to speak to their hearts about how this event could possibly fit into the message of Easter.

I began with a story about a wedding I performed in the 1980s. At the rehearsal the whole wedding party was downcast and the bride was crying. I assumed her emotion was due to the normal pre-wedding blues. As I was leaving the church to attend the rehearsal dinner, the bride and groom asked if they could talk with me. As soon as the bride entered my office and shut the door, she burst into uncontrollable tears. I asked what was wrong.

"My father just found out this morning that the biopsy report was positive," she said. "He has a malignancy. It's a fast-moving cancer, and he doesn't have long to live, and he's walking me down the aisle tomorrow."

Then the groom said, "How do you rejoice when you really want to cry?"

I told that story on Easter Sunday and repeated the question: How do you rejoice when you want to cry?

"It's been a long and hard week in Birmingham," I said. "This morning all of us sat around our breakfast tables and looked at the pictures of thirty-four people. We wept as we read the stories of people between the ages of two and eighty-nine who died this week. There's a side of us that says, 'I really find it difficult to celebrate Easter today.' But we don't have any choice. It's Easter. We're Christians, and we are supposed to rejoice."

I went on to tie our story in Birmingham with the story of the first Easter in Palestine, how it had been a devastating week in Jerusalem. The lives of three people had been taken. The lives of the disciples had been shattered. And yet there was a wonderful promise from Jesus. I had to work hard not to make the rest of the sermon a manipulative, emotional monologue. I avoided the temptation to say, "Don't you all want to be ready for Jesus when the next tornado comes?" Instead I discussed the meaning of the resurrection.

My point about the opening illustration is its placement in the sermon: at the beginning. If I had preached that same message in 1975, I might have ended the sermon with the story from the wedding. But because of the cultural shift from reason to emotion, I placed the moving story at the beginning of the sermon. I needed first to connect with my audience and then later to bring in the facts of the resurrection.

Gary Fenton is pastor of Dawson Memorial Baptist Church in Birmingham, Alabama, and author of *Your Ministry's Next Chapter*.

TUNE MY HEART TO SING THY GRACE: WHY WE PREACH FROM THE PSALMS

Lee Eclov

A fourteenth-century book on Christian prayer called The Cloud of Unknowing *says, "If we wish to quench our thirst [for God], we must lay aside books that explain thirst and take a drink." In this chapter, Lee Eclov urges, encourages, and even entices us to do just that: don't just explain the Psalms; help your people drink them, experience them, and, most important, sing them. In Eclov's words, a psalm "must be danced. It must be prayed. And the more it is prayed or sung, the deeper the meaning."*

Eclov warns that as we engage the Psalms, they might seem extreme, gushing with emotional intensity. But Eclov counters by noting that our hearts have been "drugged by inattention to God by sin and by the soul's diseases." We need some strong stuff—the Psalms, for example—to wake us up from our stupor. So there's nothing wrong with teaching your people about the forms of Hebrew poetry or the historical background on the Psalms. But, according to Eclov, by the time you get done preaching on the Psalms,

make sure your people want to drink and be satisfied. Preach on the
Psalms so your people can't wait to stand up and sing.

Preaching on a psalm is like trying to give a talk on *America*
the Beautiful or *Somewhere Over the Rainbow*. Psalms are meant
to be sung—or at least read—again and again, till we know the
next line before we read it, till we know their spiritual pitch
without a piano introduction, till our hearts naturally begin to
think and speak in psalmic.

So what's a preacher to do when our text is a psalm? We
tend toward spiritual musicology, lecturing on the song's history and structure. ("Do you see the chiasm in verses 5 and 6?")
We take the word pictures and deconstruct them, as if to help
people find the faint blue numbers under the psalmist's paint.
We rightly point out the expressions of faith or joy or pain and
try to walk our people into the music, but we end up sounding
like a documentary on how the orchestra works.

The preacher of the Psalms is like a choral conductor re-
hearsing a choir. I've directed choirs for years. I'm not great at
it, but I know my role. For one thing, I see to the choir's sound—
pitch, color, dynamics, tempo. But it is also my job to see that the
group communicates the music: that they voice the message of
the composer, that they bring the music to life. When it comes
to psalms, we preach to the choir. We help them find the text's
spirit, mood, and meaning so they can do justice to it when they
sing it, or pray it, themselves or together. We preachers have to
remember that in the end God's people sing the song. We help
them learn it and love it. Then we urge them to sing it as it was
meant to be sung.

For example, in preaching Psalm 19, the magnificent paean
to the God who speaks, our introduction could poke at our in-

clination to see God's Word as ordinary, as black type on white paper, as a thousand pages to be plowed through. Then to the point: "Our text today, Psalm 19, is an anthem to God's speech, his talk, his conversation with us. Everything about God is glorious, but our ears are dulled by too much chatter, too many newspapers and billboards, and we can't see the wonder of the conversing God. But here we have a master of worship—David—who wants not only to teach us the wonders of God's Word, but to teach us how to sing for joy at the thought of it."

Then, of course, when the sermon ends be sure there is time actually to sing of God's good Word, preferably using settings of the psalmist's own words. Perhaps something special can be done to hold high the Scriptures, symbolically and literally. In our church one thing we might do is congregational sharing: "One verse of Scripture that shines like the sun to me is . . ."

The meaning in the dance

The famous ballerina Isadora Duncan was asked what a certain ballet meant. She replied, "If I could tell you what it meant, there would be no point in dancing it." There is a problem when preachers try to tell people what a psalm means. Oh, I believe the text has an unchanging, God-intended meaning. It isn't a Rorschach inkblot open to any interpretation. Yet there is a depth of meaning, a quality of meaning, that the preacher can't describe. It must be danced. It must be prayed. And the more it is prayed or sung, the deeper the meaning. (I don't mean the psalm must be literally set to music, though I'm sure we're the poorer for our tunelessness, but that it becomes our heart song, a lyrical prayer.)

This unusual way of talking to God is the heart's true language.

If I were preaching on Psalm 91, that fortress of promised safety, I would help people see the structure and understand the more obscure word pictures. But, more important, I would talk about the scores of times I've read this psalm in hospital rooms. (It is always my first choice.) I would show verbal snapshots of these places where sickness seems to be in charge, and where the future is especially murky. I would try to convey how this psalm, read again and again in crisis situations, has taken on a deeper meaning than we can acquire from a sermon or occasional devotional reading. The deeper meaning is a more settled assurance that even relentless pain and desperate diagnoses cannot assail the heart that rests in "the shadow of the Almighty" and his refuge of promises. The point: psalms mean more—mean deeper—when we've owned them in our own experience.

In preaching the Psalms, the goal is not only to lay bare the truth of the text but also to show why it was meant to be sung or prayed, not merely said. The sin-sick lament of Psalm 51, the shepherd's walk of Psalm 23, the marching-to-Zion psalms of ascent speak of God and godliness more truly because they are poetry, and even more when they're the soul's own song. Preaching helps people hear the music in their heads and hearts, urges them to make the song their own, and helps people see how to pray this way.

Another task of the preacher is tuning hearts to the psalm's pitch. Many psalms trace a soul's progress in some circumstance of life. Psalm 4, for instance, begins,

> Answer me when I call to you,
>   O my righteous God.
> Give me relief from my distress.

It ends,

> I will lie down and sleep in peace,
>   for you alone, O LORD,
>   make me dwell in safety.

The psalm traces David's journey from distress to peace.

Imagine that this psalm is a perfectly tuned, six-stringed guitar. (It is, after all, a perfectly tuned soul song.) Our people come to church each carrying their own guitar, out of pitch from a week of rough treatment and disuse. The preacher's job is to tune their heart guitars to David's heart guitar.

So we help them tune to verse 1. The preacher might ask, "Have you ever felt like you're calling God, and he doesn't pick up? Like you keep getting his answering machine? 'Come on, God,' you say, 'pick up! I know you're there.'" In saying that, the preacher is tuning the hearts of his people to verse 1.

Can you hear in your mind a guitar player tuning her guitar? A string plucked and resonating. Then she turns the tuning key—woowwaawo—till it matches the perfect pitch. That's our goal: preaching each stanza to tune hearts to the pitch of Scripture. And when we come to the end, their souls are in tune with the psalmist's, and they're ready to sing for themselves and with all the other singers. David's psalm becomes *their* psalm. We preach in order to tune their hearts to sing God's grace.

Have you noticed that some psalms seem sort of emotionally exaggerated? Take those imprecatory psalms, for example: "May his children be fatherless and his wife a widow." I'm almost never that angry with anyone. My psalm would be much more restrained: "Lord, make those irritating people start being nice to me." At the other end of the spectrum, there is that exuberant praise: "Shout for joy to the LORD, all the earth." I don't even like clapping along with the praise songs.

But the biblical psalms aren't exaggerated. Sometimes, though, our hearts are drugged by inattention to God, by sin, and by the soul's diseases. We don't feel much of anything spiritually. Sermons on psalms remind people who hardly know the sound of their own inward voice (let alone the Holy Spirit's) what it is like when the godly pray or weep, complain or worship.

Take those loud crashing anthems at the end of the Psalms. Our problem isn't understanding those calls to worship, nor explaining why all creation ought to praise God. It is just that for many of us we can rarely imagine being that jazzed about praising God. Our task is to tantalize both mind and emotions with the glories of God so that people not only understand why everything that has breath should praise the Lord, but also so that the congregation can't wait for the songs that follow the sermon.

To do that, the preacher will have to step outside the psalm itself to the mighty deeds of God, recounting with childlike wonder the exodus, the great sun-stopping victories of God, the glories of Christ, the sweet homemaking of the Spirit in our hearts, and the enchanting hope of heaven. Tell why cedars should praise God: And you cedars, sing! Let the wind play you like great clarinets. For God gives life and beauty and fragrance, a majesty that hints at his own. He has even brought you into his very temple as the paneling of his dwelling. And if that is not enough, move on to rhapsodize about the character of the Triune God. Punctuate this recounting with the calls to worship from the psalm itself. This sermon won't fit into the three-point structure, and it will require that the preacher has summoned his own soul to profound praise before he is fit to preach.

Building a soul-song repertoire

Preaching also helps put these loud psalms in perspective. We help people see where and when this prayer will be needed. We help people prepare a soul-song repertoire for the days ahead. We may not need an angry song or an exalting anthem at this moment, but surely we will. And on that day, we won't have time to learn it. We won't want to have to hum our way through. "Why are you downcast, O my soul something, something, mmmm?" Someday their souls will need a vocabulary they seldom use, a song to let the heartbreak out or to set their God-touched spirits soaring. Preachers teach them those songs.

Not long ago I sat on a bench at sunset overlooking the Grand Canyon. People strolled along in front of me, trying to take it all in. One woman stopped, shook her head a little, and, groping for words, blurted, "Ohwhoopee!" That woman needed a psalm!

Have you ever led congregational singing and spotted folks standing there, but not singing? It's unsettling. I'd really like to stop everyone and say, "What's up with you?" Who knows? Maybe they don't know the song, or don't like to sing, or don't want anyone to hear their poor voice. But I always suspect they're dulled, distant, disconnected. They don't know that singing lifts them. I sing "Jesus is all the world to me" even when he isn't, because singing it—especially with others—makes it truer and moves me closer to where I want to be.

Preaching the Psalms draws silent, voiceless, reluctant souls to sing or pray. Some don't know that the saved soul can sing. Only unredeemed souls are tone deaf. The redeemed have a new song to sing. When we preach a psalm, we urge people to make it the lyric of their hearts. It isn't enough to tell them what it means. Our job is to set them a-singing. To set the cadences and spiritual rhymes into their memory. God's beloved people often don't know how wide and deep their songs and prayers are meant to go. When we preach the Psalms, we give them a spiritual phrasebook so they have the language to push back the frontiers of their experience with God.

A friend told me about being at a men's gathering when sixty thousand men sang, "Holy, Holy, Holy." He dialed his wife on his cell phone and whispered, "Listen to this," and then held his phone in the air. He didn't want her just to hear the song; he wanted her to hear the way it was sung. Preachers urge people to hear the way the songs of Zion are meant to be sung. And we help them understand that these are the songs of all the saints, that a great cloud of witnesses has sung them before us.

Psalms are more soulish than the rest of Scripture. They are also more responsive. Whereas the prophets and storytellers and apostles inform our ignorance and challenge our error, biblical psalms teach us to talk to God, to sing to him. It is a serious matter that so many of God's people find the Psalms to be as distant to them as the poetry of Tennyson. "I just don't get into the Psalms," they say. "I prefer the Epistles and the Gospels." But the Psalms teach us to pray. They are the Lord's Prayer writ large. We don't preach the Psalms only for their theology or their emotion, but to give God's people soul songs and a book of common prayer. We help them see that this ancient song is their today song and that this unusual way of talking to God is the heart's true language.

Selah.

Lee Eclov is pastor of the Village Church of Lincolnshire, in Lake Forest, Illinois, a consulting editor to *Leadership Journal*, and a regular contributor to PreachingToday.com.

FIVE VEINS OF DEEP PREACHING

Scott Chapman

At some point in his or her ministry, most pastors hear these un-settling words: "We want deeper sermons." As a preacher, it's sure easy to take those words as a personal assault. And it's confusing: What does it mean when people say they want "deeper sermons"?

Thankfully, Scott Chapman defuses the threat and untangles the mystery behind the request for deeper preaching. Chapman takes that phrase, pulls it apart, and patiently shows us what he calls the "five veins of deep preaching": biblical knowledge, intellectual depth, experiential depth, cultural understanding, and applica-tional depth. In the process he helps us honestly ask: How can my preaching help people grow into fully equipped followers of Christ?

Most of the time, when people want "deeper preaching" it's a posi-tive sign. As Chapman writes, "Depth adds value, sets our words apart from the background noise of our culture, and builds lasting change." When it comes to feeding our bodies, there's certainly nothing wrong with desiring a balanced diet. And when it comes to feeding souls, there's nothing wrong with helping our people grow in these five key areas of deep preaching.

Several years ago our teaching team decided it would be good for us to get some feedback from our people about our preaching. Their overwhelming response was, "We want deeper messages." I was surprised and a little taken aback by this since I felt that we already were creating reasonably deep messages. We decided to probe further by asking people what depth meant to them. Again their answers surprised and confused us. While everyone wanted deeper messages, they differed widely on what "deeper" meant. Not only were our messages missing the target for many people; they disagreed on what the target actually was.

After analyzing their responses further, though, the feedback started to make sense. We were able to group people's ideas about deeper preaching into five areas, and we began thinking through how to increase the depth of our sermons in each of these areas. As we began viewing depth as a multifaceted reality, it revolutionized the way we planned series and developed messages. Our preaching team now digs down for five aspects of sermon depth.

Biblical depth

Biblical depth focuses on exploring the primary passage of the message. This involves processing the richness of the original context, leading people through the nuances of the text, and helping them to develop a broader biblical framework by connecting the passage to other parts of Scripture. Biblical depth opens people's eyes to the value of Scripture and anchors them to the truth of God's Word. While people are generally less interested in the conjugation of Greek and Hebrew verbs and the opinions of various commentators, they do value exploring the world of the biblical writers and connecting their thoughts to the broader themes found in Scripture.

As an example of a pastor who provides biblical depth in an accessible way, I think of John Ortberg, pastor of Menlo Park Presbyterian Church in California.

We recently did a message series at our church called Kings, in which we used a Discovery Channel approach to understanding the kings of Israel and Judah. We handed our people an oversized playing card that contained the names of each king, placed on a timeline, with key pertinent information and a simple visual reference to the trajectory of their spiritual lives (e.g., a card with a spade represented a king that turned away from God; a card with heart represented a king who stayed faithful to God). This helped to make a difficult biblical history both understandable and fun.

Biblical depth matters because our words lack the capacity to transform people in the way God's Word does. No matter how thoughtful, eloquent, or persuasive our messages may be, they are only as powerful as our ability to connect the hearer to the heart of Scripture.

Intellectual depth

Intellectual depth brings added reflection to the main idea of a message, thinking through the questions, issues, and perspectives raised by the scriptural text. This depth gives greater context by connecting to a range of thought and opinion on the subject.

My tendency is to focus on the *what* of a passage (what does this passage say?) and then move quickly to the *how* (how does this work in our lives?). I easily neglect the *why* question (why

115

is this important to God? why do we struggle with this?). Intellectual depth comes from probing the *why* questions that arise from a passage of Scripture.

Of the preachers whom I regularly listen to, the ones who excel at connecting people to the *why* question are Timothy Keller, pastor of Redeemer Presbyterian Church in New York, and author and speaker Ravi Zacharias. The intellectual depth of these preachers expands people's thinking, demonstrates the depth of God's wisdom, and proves that Christian thought can not only stand alongside but also lead its secular counterparts.

Last fall we spent several weeks exploring what the fourth chapter of Philippians says about joy. Some of the *why* questions we asked were: Why do we wrestle to have joy? Why do Christians battle against depression and anxiety? Why do Christians, who believe that joy comes from God, often choose to look for it in other places? This process of working through what was behind our struggles to have joy transformed this series from an encouraging reminder to a voyage of discovery.

Experiential depth

Experiential depth opens a supernatural dynamic in the message. Strong preaching not only comments on what God had to say long ago, but it also invites him to speak in the moment. People don't just need to learn about God; they also need to experience God. One way we do that is by creating moments for hearers to become more aware of God's presence during the course of our messages. Those moments can be as simple as a time of reflection, a moment of prayer, or an activity designed to draw people into the immediate presence of God. Bill Hybels and the teaching team at Willow Creek Church in South Barrington, Illinois, are well known for providing experiential depth in their sermons.

For instance, one of my favorite services of the year is on Good Friday. We have a tradition that has become meaningful for our people. We set aside a portion of our service to reflect on our individual sins and write down the specific ways in which we have failed God over the previous year. After processing through the list with God and asking his forgiveness, every person carries their sins to a wooden cross and drives a nail through them, connecting them personally to Christ's sacrifice on their behalf. It is a transcendent, sacred moment that powerfully communicates the message of the gospel. Our history has shown that in that experience, the presence of God often touches people.

We have found that the more we create opportunities that invite God to work, the greater the work that our people experience him doing. Of course God always lives in the preaching of his Word and is active in the hearts of listeners, and we are not looking to manufacture manipulative, emotional moments. But people in our culture increasingly process life through an experiential lens. Usually the younger the congregation is, the more this holds true. Our ability to lead the next generation spiritually hinges on our capacity to connect them to the presence of God through our message.

Cultural depth

Cultural depth targets greater insight into relevant cultural issues. There is a constant flood of ideas emanating from our culture—from politics, technology, movies, books, music, mass marketing, the internet—that form a national conversation, of which our people are a part. This conversation is impacting their lives and shaping their perspective. Our role is to help people understand how the ideas of Jesus intersect with and influence that discussion. Andy Stanley, pastor of North Point Church in Atlanta, is an example of a preacher who provides cultural depth.

Last fall we did a message series called Lost in Suburbia. We understood that though suburbanites live in close proximity to one another, they are relationally isolated. We are all alone—together. We explored this phenomenon and how it connects to Jesus' teachings about relationships and community.

Too often Christians have a knee-jerk reaction to our culture—either embracing it uncritically or rejecting it without really taking the time to understand it. Thinking through the nuances of our time and place in history is an essential part of contextualizing the message of Christ in a language native to our culture. This is a pivotal choice for the church as a whole—we cannot afford to be either spiritually compromised or culturally isolated. Rather, we must find ways to preach the unchanging truth of Jesus Christ in a way the people around us can understand.

Applicational depth

Depth in sermon application provides a concrete pathway for people to integrate the ideas of the message into their everyday lives. This kind of depth is centered on specific next steps, easy-to-grasp handles, and clear how-to's—items people can act on immediately after hearing a message. As an example, David Daniels and the team at Pantego Bible Church in Fort Worth, Texas, do an exemplary job at providing depth in sermon application.

Our church emphasizes this. We regularly provide our people with take-home activities, guides, and resources to reinforce the message and help them take the first steps in making it real in their lives. Increasingly we have been finding ways to connect our message to social media such as blogs, Facebook, and Twitter to create environments that continue and expand the dialogue around how to live out our faith.

We always ask ourselves: As a result of this message, what are we asking our people to do—and how are we going to support them in it? This intention shapes the way we approach our messages. Preaching can transform people not only on the weekend, but the other six days of the week as well. By helping people make good decisions, engage in healthy behaviors, and develop life-transforming habits, we lead them toward the abundant life that God has promised to all who follow him.

Although we aim to preach with a multifaceted perspective on depth, I've found it's better to focus on one or two areas of depth in any one message. Though we cannot drill down into each area during every message, we seek to balance them out over the course of a year. In developing our preaching calendar, we not only plan the subjects, we also prayerfully consider the depth gauges of various series.

In an age when we are literally flooded with information, we need to be sure that the message of Christ has staying power with our hearers. Depth adds value, sets our words apart from the background noise of our culture, and builds lasting change. When we embrace a multifaceted understanding of depth into our preaching, we have the best chance to leave a lasting mark on the hearts of others.

Scott Chapman is senior pastor of The Chapel, in Grayslake, Illinois.

PREACHER AS ADVOCATE

John Koessler

At a low point in my ministry, an older church member took me out for lunch. As I complained about the congregation's lack of involvement, he quietly interrupted. "Let me ask one question: Do you even like us?" The question stunned me. "Of course I like this church," I said defensively. He gently said, "Your preaching makes many of us feel that you're disappointed with us. It's hard to feel inspired when we just hear what we're doing wrong."

In this chapter John Koessler describes a similar awakening: "I get the impression that I don't like the people I'm preaching to, that I'm angry with them, that they don't quite measure up." Fortunately Koessler provides a simple solution to this approach to preaching: Become an advocate for your people. The apostle Paul acted like a father to his people—encouraging, comforting, and exhorting (see 2 Thess. 2:11–12)—but they never doubted that he was on their side.

How about you? Do people know that you are for them and not against them? Even when you preach on difficult topics, urging and exhorting, would they still say, "We know that our preacher is walking with us, not just standing in judgment over us"?

Whenever you step into the pulpit, you are the advocate of the people who listen to you. You are a mediator of the text for them. You stand between the text and the people, and your role is to help them understand God's Word.

Unfortunately, in our preaching we may adopt an adversarial relationship with our hearers. It's not intentional, and it may come from a desire to preach prophetically, but some of us are more comfortable pronouncing seven woes than five blessings.

I realized this after I left pastoring and went into teaching. I took my place in the pew on Sundays and listened to sermons and realized how often I left the meeting feeling as though someone had beaten up on me. When I looked at some of my older sermons, I realized I too sometimes had an edge.

One of the older preachers who models preaching as an advocate is Helmut Thielicke, who has this wonderful series of sermons based on the Lord's Prayer in a book called *The Prayer That Spans the World.* Thielicke preached in Stuttgart during the Allied bombing of Germany during World War II. He tells about meeting one of the women in his congregation by this bombed-out building as he's walking through the city, and she points down into the crater and says, "My husband died there." So here's this pastor in a context of sheer terror, and his sermons are filled with compassion. He voices all the fears and questions his congregation has about God, but he does it with such sympathy. You can tell when he's preaching that he's on their side. He's looking at the problem through their eyes. He's not looking down on them, not scolding, not preaching from Sinai. He's like Christ, who comes and dwells among us and takes our burdens on himself.

What disturbs me when I read some of my old sermons is I get the impression that I don't like the people I'm preaching to, that I'm angry with them, that they don't quite measure up to my expectations.

At times you have to speak prophetically. You can't just say what people want to hear, but it's not the image of the prophet that makes that kind of preaching effective. Where we get hung up is in our vision of what it means to be a prophet: It's standing on the mountain and thundering at God's people. Instead, the secret to biblical, prophetic preaching is the metaphor of parent. As a parent at times I have to say hard things to my children. At times I have to say things I would rather not say and things they don't want to hear, but I am compelled by love to say them. I don't want to denounce my children.

Sometimes we fail to identify with our audience. When Thielicke preached to his people, he voiced their fear that God had abandoned them or that this wreckage was proof that he doesn't exist. Thielicke gives the sense that it's understandable they would feel that way. Then he brings the audience and the text together, showing how those fears are unfounded where Christ is concerned.

We need the ability to identify with the audience in such a way that we can speak on their behalf, and then be so grounded in the text that we also can speak for God. In a real sense the preacher is a mediator, not in the salvific way—we know Jesus is the only one who can do that—but the preacher stands between the audience and the text. When you analyze the text, you speak to the text on behalf of your audience. You think about your people, trying to look at the text through the lens of their experience, particularly the lens of their needs. You ask of the text the questions they would ask if they saw the text as you do. Then you speak to the audience on behalf of the text or, in other words, on behalf of God. You answer their questions based on the text, and you're doing that as their friend.

John Koessler is the chairman of the pastoral studies department at Moody Bible Institute in Chicago. John is general editor of *The Moody Handbook of Preaching* and author of *A Stranger in the House of God*. He is an editorial adviser to PreachingToday.com.

PREACHING WITH
CHILDLIKE WONDER

Matt Woodley

Nearly a hundred years ago the British writer G. K. Chesterton quipped, "There are no uninteresting things, only uninterested people." Chesterton disciplined his heart to experience wonder in uninteresting places. Chesterton wanted to experience the excitement of "existence in places that could be commonly called dull as ditch-water."

In this chapter I urge preachers to find the excitement in passages of Scripture that might seem common, dull, or predictable—at least on our first reading. To paraphrase Chesterton, "There are no uninteresting Scripture passages, only uninterested preachers." Of course sometimes as preachers we lose our passion due to the daily grind of pastoral ministry or the yearly cycle of preaching on the same seasonal topics and themes.

So how do we keep looking at Scripture with childlike wonder? How do we avoid a weary, blasé approach to the Bible? What are the practices of preachers who keep the joy and excitement in their preaching? They're crucial questions, because if preachers lose interest in a biblical text, there's no way our people will get inspired by the text either.

During my first pastorate in northeastern Minnesota, I befriended an older parishioner, Howard Ballou, a dairy farmer with huge hands and soft eyes. Throughout his long life (ninety-one years), Howard suffered many losses: the death of his ten-year-old son, the sale of the family-run dairy farm (and his precious Guernsey cows), the death of his wife and lifelong sweetheart. Toward the end of his life, after the reconstruction of both knees, Howard struggled and ached. The once-strong dairyman who worked fourteen-hour days now clung to his aluminum walker with each painful step. At times his body and his spirit shook with sadness.

But until his last breath, one thing Howard never lost: his almost childlike sense of wonder.

When I visited Howard six months before his death, he had a Bible (open to Leviticus 13) and a *TV Guide* perched on his lap.

"Howard," I asked, "what are you doing with Leviticus and *TV Guide*?" Howard chuckled and said, "God is so amazing. I'm reading my Bible from cover to cover, and I'm watching all the nature shows I can. I still have so much to learn."

At the age of ninety-one, Howard lived before God with unquenchable wonder.

As preachers it's sometimes easy to lose our wonder for God's Word. After a while we can approach the Bible like a guy I knew who was planning another sailing trip around the Caribbean. He nonchalantly told me, "Yeah, next week I'll be sailing the Caribbean again—for the fifth time. Sure, it's beautiful—crystal clear ocean, blue skies, hot sun, white sandy beaches, warm wind in your face—but how many times can you see the same stuff? I mean, it's nice, but it just gets a little wearisome. It's such a burden sometimes."

I wanted to grab the guy and say, *Are you nuts? Dude, how about if I take your place? Why don't you just lay your "burden" down, and I'll carry it for you?*

Sadly, sometimes we approach Bible texts like this dullard. *Been there, done that. Yeah, I've read Exodus before. Sure (yawn), I preached the resurrection last year. Well, I guess I have to do Romans again.*

How much better to talk about God's Word in a way that's fresh and alive. Then we can also ask the Holy Spirit to enable our people to hear God's Word with amazement—even if they've heard this text a dozen times before. How do we do that? How do we live before God and then preach as one fully alive?

Learn from wonder-filled people

I love to study writers who, like Howard Ballou, live with a spirit of freshness and joy. These authors heal my wonder deficiency so I can see a biblical text with fresh eyes. The twentieth-century Jewish writer Abraham Joshua Heschel helped me recover a sense of reverence for God. He used a simple phrase that captures our response to the mystery of God—he called it "radical astonishment." For Heschel, "The beginning of happiness lies in understanding that a life without wonder is not worth living." I want to recapture that spirit every time I open the Bible to preach.

I've also learned from Lewis Thomas, a scientist and physician who argued that "the more we learn, the more we are—or ought to be—dumbfounded." In his essay "On Bewilderment," after describing how the first brain cell appears in the human body, Thomas effused, "All the information needed for learning to read and write, playing the piano, or the marvelous act of putting out one hand and leaning against a tree, is contained in that first cell."

No one knows why an ordinary human cell turns into a brain cell. It just does. Thomas concluded his essay on a note of praise: "If anyone succeeds in explaining it within my lifetime, I will charter a skywriting airplane, maybe a whole fleet of them, and send them aloft to write out one great exclamation point after another, until my money runs out."

That challenges me as I prepare to preach. I want to approach the Bible with a similar sense of awe. God does indeed have something amazing to say to his people this week through this text.

Dig for the awesome

Finding the awesome doesn't just happen. I usually have to work at finding the wonder in each text.

Let's say I'm preaching on a familiar passage (e.g., the Lord's Prayer or Psalm 23 or John 3:16) or a difficult passage (e.g., Judges 3, where Ehud assassinates Eglon). Part of my job is to keep reading the text, meditating on it, savoring it, until I'm able to draw nourishment from its richness. That richness is there. God's Word is more to be desired than gold, and sweeter than the honeycomb (Ps. 19:10). If it looks bland or even bitter, that may have to do with the condition of my heart—or it's just a hard passage to preach. Or perhaps the Word of God looks blasé because I haven't dug into its depths. My role as a preacher is to keep digging, keep praying, keep looking at the Scripture until the honey starts oozing out.

I love the attitude of G. K. Chesterton, who once claimed that the entire spiritual life hinges on this choice to see God's wonders. In his autobiography, Chesterton writes that on his journey to Christ, he found "a forgotten blaze or burst of astonishment at our own existence." It became clear to him that the entire goal of the "artistic and spiritual life was to dig for this submerged sunrise of wonder."

This is one of the glad duties of the preacher: to keep digging into a text—prayerfully, attentively, expectantly—until I strike the submerged sunrise of wonder.

Regain the childlike

But this won't come to just anyone. There's a certain inner disposition that allows us to keep digging and then to keep finding the beauty of God's Word. Jesus put it this way: "Truly I tell you, unless you change and become like little children, you will never enter the kingdom of heaven" (Matt. 18:3).

In terms of our salvation, that means that we can't buy or earn our way to God; we have to accept it as a free gift. But this childlike attitude needs to continue throughout our entire life with Jesus.

We're always in danger of missing the wonder of God's Word whenever we assume that as a grown-up we completely understand it all. *I've got this down*, we boast. *I've read this twenty times. I've preached on this three times. I know what this text means.* But every time I approach a Bible text, the Holy Spirit is working in my life in a different place. My congregation is in a different place, in a different season. The basic meaning of the text might be the same, but I can always see things from an angle that I never noticed before.

129

I want to come to the text with the humility of a beginner rather than the pomposity of a know-it-all. I want to come with openness and expectancy, as if I'm reading this text for the first time. That's the key to finding the element of surprise in every Bible passage.

For example, I've been thinking about "Blessed are the poor in spirit, for theirs is the kingdom of heaven" (Matt. 5:3) for years. But recently, after I went through a profound encounter with my own spiritual poverty, I now see that verse from a different vantage point. The meaning of the text remains the same, but my grasp of that meaning is deeper, richer, and tinged with more pain and joy.

In a similar way, when I was younger, I preached on suffering, but my sermons were more abstract and theoretical. Then after walking through a season of suffering, people commented that my sermons on suffering suddenly came alive.

Sometimes when people ask, "How long did it take to prepare that sermon?" I want to say, "Oh, about twenty years."

Ask God to make dry bones live

Of course this isn't something that we can do just by trying. We don't pump ourselves up so we sound excited about this particular passage. I usually begin every week with a text that, in all honesty, looks like Ezekiel's valley of dry bones. Every time I approach such a text, the Lord asks me, "Can these dry bones live?" and I respond, "Only you know, Lord" (which usually means, "You've got to be kidding, Lord").

In other words, every week I look at the text and pray: "Lord, if you don't do a miracle with these dry bones, this sermon will just stay dry and dead." Dead bones can never produce life. Only God can give life.

So sermons never start with *my* inspiration or *my* excitement or *my* ability to say something fresh or interesting. No, it's about God's ability to do a miracle and bring life to this sermon, transforming my words into the words of God for those who hear. Ultimately that's my only hope as a preacher.

In one sense God wants to open our hearts to the wonder of the entire gospel, not just one biblical text or theme. For instance, just to know that God would come and die for us even while we were still sinners—that's utterly outlandish and incomprehensible. It's such lavish love. We didn't deserve it, and there's no way we could have seen it coming.

But God did it for us. How should we respond to that? By letting "radical astonishment" wash all over our souls. Should we rent a fleet of skywriting airplanes and write "God loves you" until our money runs out? I suppose that's one way to respond. But here's our amazing privilege: as preachers, each week we get to do something better than rent skywriting airplanes. We get to dig for the submerged sunrise of wonder in God's Word. We get to taste his Word and see that God is good.

Then we get to stand up and declare the beauty and glory of our God—and we can do it all for free.

Matt Woodley has served churches in Minnesota and on Long Island and authored *The Folly of Prayer* and *The Gospel of Matthew: God With Us*. He is the managing editor of PreachingToday.com.

LAST SUNDAY YOU PREACHED YOUR FINAL BORING SERMON

Michael Quicke

Imagine you've just sat down to watch a new movie, an action thriller loaded with unpredictable plot twists. But as the movie starts, your friend leans over and says, "I just saw this film last week. Just so you know, in the last scene . . ." and then he proceeds to tell you exactly how the movie will end. By sharing the entire plotline, your friend has removed all the surprises and basically ruined the movie for you.

Michael Quicke argues that preachers will lose their listeners if they continually preach with "bone-crushing" predictability. Inspiring sermons, like good movies or interesting stories of all kinds, need what Quicke calls "startling details that shock and challenge the hearer." Quicke provides a helpful guide on how you can preach what he calls "your last boring sermon."

More than anything, Quicke urges us to be bold in how we challenge people with God's Word. As the twentieth-century spiritual writer Thomas Merton once said, "Do not be like one of those [preachers], who rather than risk failure, never attempts anything."

In other words, take risks for God, be bold for God, and then bring the passage home and make it stick.

I remember witnessing a particularly slow death in the pulpit. After a lively worship service, the preacher stood up to read Isaiah 6:1–8. Then he said, "Isaiah lived in Jerusalem in 740 B.C." He spent about five minutes setting the scene and explaining background about King Uzziah. Then he asked us to note three points. First, Isaiah saw God in the temple. Second, Isaiah heard God in the temple. And third (can you guess it?), Isaiah obeyed God in the temple.

Judging by the restlessness and yawns all around me, I was not alone in being able to predict each step before the preacher got to it. We reached the end long before the preacher did. The problem was not that the preacher had been short on preparation, nor that he was insincere. It was that he was utterly, bone-crushingly predictable.

Even the best news people can ever hear can lose interest fast if it becomes predictable good news. As soon as people know what we are going to say next and how we are going to say it, and are proved right, we are in trouble.

Of course one can argue that a measure of predictability is built into biblical preaching. If a Scripture text is well known, like Isaiah 6, then a faithful preacher will surely have a large dose of predictability built into the sermon.

One can also argue that congregations do not need shock tactics from whiz-bang preachers who feel they always need to be different. The continuous search for novelty is a sure way to superficiality. God calls biblical preachers not to be original but to be faithful.

But Scripture is rarely predictable in the exact ways it makes impact today. A high doctrine of the inspiration of Scripture involves belief not only that the Holy Spirit breathed it into existence but also that he continues to breathe its interpretation for today. It is a living word, sharper than a two-edged sword, so full of God's dynamism that you never know where it will cut and how it will make impact.

Our sermons will convey that dynamism if they have the following qualities, as illustrated by the Isaiah text.

See the full riches in the text

A careful reading of Scripture is almost never without surprises. Predictability comes from a tired approach to Scripture that reads it flatly in order to get a workable outline as fast as possible. Predictability comes when we assume we know the text.

The sermon on Isaiah 6 failed on this account in three ways: (1) It stopped at verse 8, cutting out the controversial and interesting material in 6:9–13. (2) It seemed stuck on Isaiah's story. Of course history matters, but the sermon focused exclusively on what happened to him without getting inside this stunning spiritual event for the listener today. (3) It settled on three obvious aspects of Isaiah's response.

Although familiar, this Bible story actually brims over with startling details that shock and challenge the hearer.

Have a truly big idea

Big ideas capture the imagination. Big ideas make people think. Big ideas stretch people in unpredictable ways. Until we are excited about the main thing this sermon will say and do, we probably do not yet have a truly big idea. In place of a big idea, the plod through Isaiah's story simply recounted what happened to Isaiah.

Here is a big idea that would make for a less predictable sermon: Our God has the right to interrupt you and send you out on a tough calling—perhaps today.

Emphasize application

Bryan Chapell calls application the sermon's breaking point and says it is the most difficult part of preaching. Why? Because this is where the word hits home in the lives of real people. A sermon in Isaiah 6 can make some good general points about God's holiness and the need for cleansing or about obeying God's call. But as soon as the message gets personal, it becomes uncomfortable. Precise, concrete, daringly applied promises, rebukes, and challenges are what cause believers to grow—and what make for sermons that are anything but boring.

The opening sermon on Isaiah 6 was sadly weak in application, because it blandly retold a familiar story and asked listeners to draw their own conclusions. It was easy for the uncommitted to shrug their shoulders and say, "So what?" The sermon conveyed none of the shock of being confronted by the holy God and of overhearing the call to mission as a contemporary possibility. By contrast, specific application makes the present, interrupting call of God a live possibility.

Use a variety of sermon forms

Most preachers develop habits in their sermon form that provide a comfort zone. We may design a structure of "three heads and nine tails" with a gift for alliteration. We may move from story to story with a looser structure. Preachers become known for their style and length, and many congregations value the security of a predictable format and length.

But a rut too is predictable. We need to step out of our comfort zones and dare to proclaim God's big ideas in fresh ways.

We can preach Isaiah 6, for example, in many forms:

- Verse-by-verse exposition. For those who major in topical preaching, this is an excellent change of pace.

- Thematic preaching. This text has many great themes, such as the call, the preacher's task, and God's tough mission—each of which can be a sermon.

- Narrative preaching. Retell the Isaiah story as though it were contemporary. Begin by describing a worship service familiar to the listeners. Set the scene in their experience. Surprise them with how God views uncleanness today and calls for action now.

- Surprise-plotted preaching. Set up a shock in the sermon. Tell the story so it ends at verse 8. Stop and ask whether anything else happens. Let the hard realism of verses 9–13 surprise the listeners. What is going on here? Why did the story not finish at verse 8? What are the lessons of rejection for Isaiah, Jesus, and us?

By exploring and developing these avenues for preaching, you can see the surprise in the text and then convey that suspense to your listeners. You don't have to preach with dull predictability, After all, the Word of God is far from predictable or dull. Capture the surprise in what the text meant back then, and then let your hearers catch the surprise in the text as well. We can hope that last Sunday really was your last boring sermon!

Michael Quicke is professor of preaching at Northern Baptist Seminary in Lombard, Illinois, and author of *360-Degree Preaching*.

A GOOD MYSTERY

Richard Hansen

The Christian fiction writer Flannery O'Connor once wrote, "Mystery is an embarrassment to the modern mind." According to Richard Hansen, mystery might embarrass some preachers too. In some ways we feel pressured to tie up every loose end, answer every tough question, and resolve every tension and paradox—all in a thirty-minute sermon.

But Hansen contends that allowing some room for mystery can actually benefit our people. For Hansen mystery refers to the parts of our faith that "don't fit together in neat ways." For instance, how do you take profound theological paradoxes—such as the Trinity or the dual natures of Christ—and wrap them up in tidy formulas or neat three-point sermons? You can't—and that's okay. As a matter of fact, mystery can drive us deeper into a life of worship.

Hansen certainly isn't against providing solid biblical conclusions in our preaching. But in this chapter he'll argue, "We preachers do our people a disservice if we don't introduce them to the paradox and mystery of our faith, particularly when so much of our faith comes in paradox." Too much "how-to" preaching can leave our

*people feeling spiritually anemic. At times it's best to let people
gnaw on the rich meat of mystery.*

Many cultural experts say postmodernists respond to
preaching with an element of mystery. Several years ago I explored this theme in an article for *Leadership Journal*. On its
simplest level, mystery means that there's a lot of the landscape
of human life that is beyond our understanding. The American
poet Carl Sandburg once said that there is an eagle in me that
wants to soar, and there's a hippopotamus in me that wants to
wallow in the mud. That describes our human condition. The
apostle Paul describes it pretty well in Romans 7. So by *mystery*
I mean all those elements of human life and also the Christian
faith that don't fit together in neat ways. What I don't mean by
mystery is just the absurd. Paradox has a certain sense of tension
to it; even though it can't be rationally separated, much of the
truth we have comes to us in that form. It comes to us in the
form of two different truths that are held together in tension.

For example, consider this mystery and paradox: God is three
and yet one, the mystery of the Trinity. Or consider this: Jesus is
fully human and yet fully God, the mystery of incarnation. Or
consider the nature of our salvation: It's totally by God's grace,
and yet we have to personally respond in faith in order to receive
it. The mystery of divine providence and human free will. Our
whole lives are shot through with mystery, and postmodernism
is rediscovering that. The Enlightenment world, what's called
the modernist mind-set, wanted to control life. Any of those
pieces of life that weren't controlled by human intelligence were
shoved to the margins or swept under the rug. Postmodernism
is now open to all of those elements of mystery. In some ways
that is a great boon for Christians, because we're sitting on the

mother lode of all mystery in God. We have a great opportunity to proclaim mystery in ways that people all around us are going to connect with, even better than they did decades ago.

Everyone hungers for mystery

There is a felt need to get beyond "how-to" preaching; people have a need to go deeper. That's not to say people don't have felt needs for how to be a better parent, how to have a better marriage, or how to live an emotionally fulfilling life; but people also need to grapple with questions of existence that just won't go away. That goes across all generational lines.

For example, I recently finished a series of sermons called Thorns in the Flesh: Questions That Get under Your Skin. I asked our people to send me questions about issues that have been bugging them, that they lay awake at night thinking about. I got lots of these questions, and by far the majority were not the pragmatic how-do-I-have-a-better-life?-type questions. They were questions like: How do you reconcile creation and science? Or: If someone is sinning and unrepentant, would forgiving them be accepting evil? Even though postmodernism is more associated with the Gen-X generation, people have an appetite for mystery. It's in all of us.

Of course this leads some people to ask me, "But what about those generations that find that kind of thing unsettling? They want resolution. How does that come across to them?"

We have to be wise in how we approach them. Certainly you can damage people's faith if you leave them with lots of unanswered questions when they're used to resolution, used to having all their puzzle pieces fit together. Yet life is like having some puzzle pieces on the table that you don't quite know where to fit. Our preaching should leave some unanswered questions and a few loose ends dangling. Jesus was a master at this. If we're going to take Jesus as our preaching model, think of all the times he gave a sermon, and then his disciples would come later and ask, "Now what were you saying? What's the deal about the soil?" And he would explain it to them. In some ways, preachers today have been brainwashed into thinking we have to give people 100-percent answers, that they can't handle loose ends. Yet Jesus did that all the time. He did it in ways that helped people keep growing in their journey.

How to preach the paradoxes of the Bible

There are several things I've discovered along the journey. We need to be more willing to leave people with some dangling questions and not unnecessarily give them all the answers. Sometimes that's being honest with ourselves as preachers and saying, "I don't have all the answers." I've tried to be transparent about my own doubts and questions and confusions.

Another thing I try to do that has been helpful is not to take everything quite so seriously. There is a real element of playfulness in mystery, and I see that in Jesus. He says paradoxical things to get people outside of their boxes. So I try to be playful at times.

For example, on one occasion I tried to preach about the paradox of the Lord's Supper: It's a serious event, and yet it's also a party, a banquet. How do those two things fit together? So I created an imaginary story about famous Christian thinkers throughout history—even a serious theologian like John Calvin—who will be serving at the messianic banquet at the end of history. During the sermon these thinkers ask us if we really understood the joy of the Lord's Supper. My message wasn't a frontal attack on being too serious about the Lord's Supper or a grim message about how you must be more joyful. Instead, throughout the sermon I told an imaginary story with a biblically based underlying message about the joy of Communion. Oftentimes playfulness can introduce people in a nonthreatening way into these elements of mystery.

Another thing I've discovered is that traditional paradoxes can be put together in fresh ways to heighten this element of tension. In the examples I gave earlier—God is three and yet one, and Jesus is fully human and yet fully God, our salvation is predestined and yet there is free will—all of these have an inherent tension. Most of the truths we have as Christians are held in these tensions. To me preaching paradox is not a matter of explaining paradox to people; it's a matter of helping them feel the tensions. If they live in that tension, not only do they come into more contact with truth, but they also have doors open into how awesome God is, that God is so much larger than can be contained in propositional truths. So I highlight these tensions.

For example, I call the tension of predestination and free will a *harmonious tension*. It's like a tuning fork. You need the two tines of the tuning fork vibrating in unison before you hear the note. There's no such thing as a one-tine tuning fork. When I preached about that tension, it was back in the days when my kids were watching *Sesame Street*. That show featured a two-headed monster that teaches kids phonics by one head saying one syllable and the other head saying the second syllable. I started at different sides of our platform, and I talked about some passages on predestination. Then I walked to the other side of the platform and talked about free will. Then I repeated that process over again—speaking from the predestination side and then speaking from the free-will side. Gradually I shortened the distance until at the end of the sermon I was in the middle saying, "This is a mystery, and we need to live in the tension of it." Instead of having a sermon on each, I used this visible way to bring them together.

Trusting God when it isn't clear

On the one hand, I certainly wouldn't dispute that it's important to have clarity in preaching. But there's also an element of our faith that won't ever provide total clarity. I like to call this conscious ignorance. I've got a story to describe that.

When we first moved to the central valley in California, it was wintertime. It doesn't snow here, but they have this thick fog called Tooley Fog. We'd been here about a week, and a family in our church who lived outside our town asked us out to dinner. It was a foggy night. They said, "You sure you don't need directions? It's very foggy." We'd come from Chicago, and we thought, *What's a little fog? These California wimps.* We started off toward their house, and this fog got thicker and thicker. Soon we were lost, and we actually drove all the way around the town without finding this house, most of the time not knowing where we were at all.

I've lived here fifteen years now, and I've learned to enjoy the fog, because it has an element of mystery to it. When you're driving into the fog, you see where the range of your headlights shines, but you realize there is a lot of area outside the range of your headlights. In other words, there's something vast out there that you can't see. That's a key element of mystery. It's this relation of the known to the unknown. Something isn't mysterious if it's completely known.

Besides being clear about what we know, we also need to be clear about what we don't know. As we do that, we have an opportunity to help people grow in their faith, because faith, classically defined, is a combination of knowledge and trust. So faith contains an element of trusting that God is faithful in what we don't know. As we come into a greater sense of what we don't know, our appreciation of how awesome God is increases, because we have to trust.

The place of how-to sermons

Certainly there's nothing wrong with how-to sermons. The how-to format came about as a way of marketing the faith, primarily to the boomer generation that was looking for answers. But if all you do is provide people with "answers," they never get beyond a utilitarian faith. Christian faith becomes a technique, and even God can become a means to my end. I worship God—not because God is awesome and holy and wonderful—but because if I learn these certain spiritual techniques, I can create a better life for myself.

Someone wrote me a letter after my article on mystery was published in *Leadership Journal*. The person said she had wrestled with some paradoxes in her own life: How could all things work together for good when she kept messing everything up with her free will? How could God work out his plan in the universe if I have a free will? If I disobey God, do I ruin his plan for my life? This person went on to say she talked with several friends about these issues, and her friends responded with, "You think too much," or, "Just don't ask questions. Take these things by faith."

In her own words she came away from that struggle "with a greater sense of how awesome God is and a strange sort of comfort stemming from the fact that I could not get my arms around God. I was finally able to rest in the fact that there is a God and I am not he." She said, "What peace I gained from that knowledge. However, if I had not struggled, I would have never come to know that peace and comfort as well as a deeper knowledge of God."

That's what I'm shooting for. People need to struggle and wrestle with the paradoxical landscape of faith. Our faith is not an interstate across Death Valley. It's a lot more like a mountain road winding its way up Pike's Peak. As we're on that road, if we can be honest about it and struggle with it, doors open into God's awesome presence, and we get the sort of comfort that this woman described: There is a God, and I am not he.

Why people need mystery in their faith

I don't think you avoid practical application. You just think of the practical application in different ways. The words *practical application* speak of a sermon that leads you to a conclusion where you say, "Okay, now do this." It's a top-down, deductive sermon. "These are the three things you should do in your life based on what's been said." But there's another method of application, and that's an inductive way, where you start with the reality of human existence.

The difference is that here you leave the door more open for people to make their own applications. You can do that by suggesting things: "It could be this, or it could be this." The practical application is still there; it's just not done deductively: "Based on what I said, here are the three things you should work on this week."

When people get engaged in the notion that paradox is a part of the landscape of our faith, it gives them a much greater comfort level in coping with the challenges of life. Again and again I've heard stories of people growing up in a conservative, evangelical home and church where they thought they had all the answers. Their faith was a complete, perfect topographical map for life, and all they had to do was follow that map. Then they went away to college, and they were thrown some things in a class that don't fit that map. They would have a friend who turns out to be a homosexual or a friend who had an abortion. Suddenly nothing seemed cut-and-dried anymore. Sadly, many of these people end up losing their faith, because they didn't have an inoculation of mystery or doubt as they were growing up. They never were told: There are parts of the faith you aren't going to be able to comprehend intellectually, and it doesn't all fit together as neatly as you might think.

An opportunity to wrestle with these things within the safety of the Christian community gives people a shot of mystery. So when they get out there in the world, they're not completely blown away by how life is. They leave the greenhouse and get out into temperatures that vary widely, and it's hard for them to thrive. We preachers do our people a disservice if we don't introduce them to the paradox and mystery of our faith, particularly when so much of our faith comes in paradox. If we can help our people grapple with that in safe ways, they are much less likely to be thrown for a loop when they confront mystery in life.

Richard P. Hansen is the former pastor of First Presbyterian Church in Visalia, California.

RED-PILL PREACHING

Mark Batterson

Recent studies have shown that most people use a metaphor every ten to twenty-five words. In other words, it's tough to have an ordinary conversation without using pictures to convey our ideas. Metaphors aren't just linguistic frills; they're at the center of normal communication.

Mark Batterson wants us to apply this natural metaphor-making instinct to our preaching. Of course he's not telling us to remake or revise the gospel; Batterson simply urges us to tell the familiar gospel story in an unforgettable way. Use fresh images. Employ daring metaphors. Keep looking at the Scripture until you see it from an exciting new perspective.

The American poet Emily Dickinson once wrote that "the truth must dazzle." That doesn't imply that the preacher has to dazzle everyone. It just means that "the most important truths ought to be communicated in the most unforgettable way." As Batterson has demonstrated in his own ministry in Washington, D.C., preachers can be "biblically sound and culturally relevant." It isn't always easy. It takes work. But in the end it's worth it to tell old truths in new ways. For preachers of God's Word there's just too much at stake.

A few months ago I was invited to speak at a twenty-something conference. I was driving north on Interstate 95 listening to a CD when I heard something totally deflating if you're a preacher by trade: "Studies indicate that we forget 95 percent of what we hear within three days."

And that's if your sermon was good!

I felt like doing an illegal U-turn and driving home. I remember praying this seventy-miles-per-hour prayer (with my eyes open): "God, I don't want to invest my time and energy saying things that people are just going to forget anyway. Help me say things in unforgettable ways!"

Unforgettable. To say things in such an anointed way that hearers don't just remember. They can't forget!

I have a simple conviction: The most important truths ought to be communicated in the most unforgettable ways.

The Red Pill

There is a riveting scene in the blockbuster movie *The Matrix* where Neo meets Morpheus for the first time. Morpheus gives Neo a choice between two pills: *You take the blue pill, and the story ends. You wake up in your bed, and you believe whatever you want to believe.*

Unfortunately, that's what happens with most messages in most churches on most Sundays. People pop the blue pill. They may be inspired or convicted or challenged by a message, but they go to bed Sunday night and get up Monday morning, and they can't remember a single word said.

But Morpheus gives Neo another option: *You take the red pill, and you stay in Wonderland, and I show you how deep the rabbit-hole goes.*

That's the goal. Get people to pop the red pill and go down the rabbit-hole of faith.

Brand truth

Here in six words is my philosophy of preaching: say old things in new ways.

In the book *In Their Time*, Anthony J. Mayo and Nitin Nohria cite one common denominator among all great leaders. "They possessed an **acute sensitivity** to the social, political, technological, and demographic contexts that came to define their eras." Mayo and Nohria call it "contextual intelligence." After studying a thousand leaders, they came to the conclusion that contextual intelligence is "an underappreciated but all-encompassing differentiator between success and failure."

If there was a way to measure contextual intelligence, Jesus would be off the charts. No one was better at recontextualization. He said, "You have heard that it was said . . . but I tell you." Jesus repackaged old covenant truths in new covenant ways.

Truth is kaleidoscopic. It is multilayered and multidimensional. And sometimes a new angle on an ancient truth can result in *metanoia*—a paradigm shift. A new angle can reveal new patterns.

I recently did a series titled The Physics of Faith. Each message revolved around a law of physics familiar to anyone who has taken Physics 101. I used Heisenberg's uncertainty principle, Bell's theorem, and the second law of thermodynamics to frame spiritual truth. I believe every "ology" is a branch of theology. We should cross-pollinate with different disciplines. If all truth is God's truth, then we need to redeem scientific research and leadership theory and cultural trends and use them to serve God's purposes.

The old real-estate adage—location, location, location—adapted to the realm of communication is metaphor, metaphor, metaphor. In *De Poetica* Aristotle said, "The greatest thing by far is to be the master of metaphor." Jesus set the standard. He used agrarian metaphors to frame truth because he knew that most of his listeners spent most of their day in the fields. He used familiar metaphors to brand truth. We call them parables.

We try to brand every message series with an organizing metaphor. The organizing metaphor for our most recent series, On Mission, was a customized passport that was so authentic it could probably have gotten you through Customs! And for our next series, Wired, we'll use wireless technology to talk about increasing spiritual bandwidth. As we begin a series called Fuel, we're buying gas station relics for staging at our coffeehouse on Capitol Hill.

The key to branding various message series is redeeming metaphors that are on the frontal lobe of cultural consciousness.

Three core convictions are the driving engine behind National Community Church, and all three affect my preaching:

C1: The church ought to be the most creative place on the planet.

C2: The greatest message deserves the greatest marketing.™

C3: The church is called to compete in the marketplace of ideas.

Irrelevance is irreverence

The key to unforgettable preaching is packaging truth in ways that are biblically sound and culturally relevant. Let me borrow from the parable of the wineskins. Think of biblical exegesis as the wine. Think of cultural relevance as the wineskin.

If you have one without the other, you're not going to quench anybody's thirst. You need the substance (biblical exegesis) and the container (cultural relevance).

If we divorce biblical exegesis and cultural exegesis, we end up with dysfunctional truth. It doesn't do anybody any good. Either we answer questions no one is asking, or we give the wrong answers.

National Community Church has a core value: Irrelevance is irreverence. God isn't just omniscient, omnipresent, and omnipotent. He's omnirelevant. He knows the number of hairs on our head. He knows every need before we verbalize it. No one is more relevant than God. So anything less than relevance is irreverence! Relevance = Reverence. Cultural relevance doesn't mean dumbing down or watering down the truth. It's about incarnating timeless truth in timely ways.

Two of our hardest-hitting series each year are two of the most relevant: God @ the Billboards and God @ the Box Office. The 60 percent of Americans who don't attend church get their theology from movies and music. So we redeem popular songs and popular movies by juxtaposing them with Scripture. We literally roll out the red carpet during God @ the Box Office and treat everyone who comes through our doors as if they're a celebrity.

Red-carpet treatment doesn't hurt when your goal is getting people to pop the red pill.

Mark Batterson is lead pastor of National Community Church in Washington, D.C., and author of *Wild Goose Chase*.

LEADING AND PREACHING

Paul Borden

Preachers are also leaders. So every time you preach, you're also inspiring a church to move forward. As Paul Borden states, "The leader communicates the vision and then asks the community to take a risk."

As the leader-preacher (or preaching leader) of a church, you have only two options: (1) lead your church to stagnation and slow death or (2) lead your church to new growth as you disciple and evangelize. Week in and week out, preaching leaders are always casting a positive, Christ-centered vision for spiritual vitality.

In this interview Borden outlines some practical steps that should shape your preaching as you lead your church. Make a plan for how you will cast the vision through your sermons. Tell lots of stories about people who are living the vision for growth. Remain positive and encourage your congregation. Ask "so what?" questions throughout your sermon. Understand the culture God has planted you in. Communicate the Bible so unbelievers and new believers can understand it and apply it. As you incorporate these themes into your preaching, you'll also be leading your people toward spiritual vitality.

What are the unique preaching challenges of strong, visionary leaders?

The primary challenges relate to the pastor's role. Seminaries have historically trained pastors to function as chaplains, responsible for preaching, counseling, and pastoral care. As a result, one of the reasons so few churches grew past three hundred prior to the 80s was because that was the most a person in that role could deal with. The church growth movement, however, began to change the paradigm of the pastor's role. If the church is going to be focusing outward, touching an unchurched culture, then the pastor has to take on a different role: the role of leader.

Our churches have also assumed that a shepherd functions like a chaplain, caring for a group of sheep. The biblical model, however, portrays a shepherd as an entrepreneur, who led sheep by still waters and into green pastures so that he could eventually shear them or kill them. In other words, he moved the sheep into zones of comfort to prepare them for zones of discomfort.

Very few pastors hold this concept of shepherding. Yet that's the role of a leader. The leader communicates the vision and then asks the community to take a risk.

This new paradigm must present several challenges.

Yes. The first one is the preacher's responsibility to communicate vision. How do you do this on a regular basis if you're busy preaching on Romans?

A second challenge is the leader's responsibility for the overall recruitment of lay people. He or she is the point person when it comes to motivating, encouraging, and making the vision exciting enough that people want to participate. Those who excel in this role recognize it as more than a once-a-year task.

Third, leaders face the constant challenge of finding needed resources. Our responsibility to be stewards in every area necessitates the leader's regular attention to this theme. Finding resources involves preaching on the stewarding of all we have, whether money, time, or talent.

The challenge is: How do you face these unique demands of leadership in light of the traditional chaplain model, with its emphasis on care giving and teaching? How do you continue to do those things while consistently fulfilling your role as a leader?

Do you have some concrete suggestions for each of these key areas? For example, how do you see responsibilities such as vision being worked out best in the pulpit?

Vision is primarily communicated through stories, specifically the stories of the people in the church who are living out the vision. This is true because story not only communicates information but also volition and emotion. When I tell someone a story as opposed to an illustration, they not only understand the point, but they also see how other people have lived it out. It touches them at an emotive and volitional level.

Vision is also communicated through a positive persona. The pastors who are most successful are also the most positive. Negativity and guilt pour out of me like sweat on a hot day. I don't have to work at that. Being positive, however, is something I must work at. For people to buy into a vision that is bigger than themselves, there has to be communication from a positive leader.

Finally, visionaries preach to the community as opposed to the individual. This is contrary to how I was trained. Visionaries ask the larger questions such as, "What does the community do for families? What does the community do for prayer? What does the community do for Bible study?" They ask the "so what?" question of the text and then answer it in the plural.

So telling stories, being positive, and preaching to the community all relate to the preacher's role as a visionary.

Would you offer some suggestions related to another task, lay mobilization?

Lay mobilization occurs as the vision is communicated. It happens as individuals are allowed to figure out how their own individual responsibilities relate to their gifts and to where the community is going. Churches that get past the 20/80 rule have a system in place capable of taking people from the pew to actual engagement once the preacher gets done preaching about lay mobilization.

The most famous of these systems is Rick Warren's baseball diamond. It says to the individual, "We want you, and will help you all along the way." The more exciting the vision, the more necessary it is to provide a system that says, "When you get done hearing me challenge you to become part of our vision, we've got people in the back of the church who are going to help you do X, Y, and Z. So sign up here." It's not just the preaching that accomplishes this task. There must also be a system in place so the person is not left hanging when the sermon is done.

Let's focus on preachers as they prepare their sermons. How does someone who is an expository or topical preacher, preaching week after week, plan his or her preaching calendar in a way that builds the church in all areas?

You need to plan your yearly calendar with your responsibilities as the leader clearly in mind. When am I going to address the issues of vision, recruitment, and raising resources?

When am I going to address exegeting our culture? When am I going to show how we as a community should reach outside of ourselves to impact the world? The churches most successful in doing outreach are those that have the best understanding of their local culture.

Regarding preaching style, if I'm going to preach with integrity from a topical perspective, I need to preach topical expository sermons. These communicate a practical message that really has its foundation in the heart and fiber of Scripture. They take five or six major passages, for example, and present a grand theme of the Scriptures that relates to where the church is and what it should be doing. The messages are deeply rooted, however, in textual study that has sound exegetical basis.

If I'm committed to an exegetical book-by-book approach, every time I make a point, I need a positive story of how average, ordinary Christians have lived this out. Steer away from stories about preachers, missionaries, or dear old sainted lay people of the church. Use story after story of real-life people. And make the stories positive.

Get to the "so what?" question of the text, and how it relates to the community. When the apostle Paul used the word *you*, it was in the plural. He was writing to the community. Likewise, you should be asking your community, "How is our church, be it First Baptist or First Presbyterian, to live this truth out?"

Finally, preach on the assumption that the people want to do it. I preach very few sermons where I beat the people over the head. In fact, I used to take one sermon a year and do nothing but compliment the congregation. I want the congregation to come out of there saying, "Yes, I can do it. God saved me. He's given me the ability. He's given me the motivation." To me, the greatest compliment I can get after a sermon is, "Hey, that was motivating."

Talk a little more about exegeting your culture and reaching out.

I believe the church works with three cultures. It works with a national culture such as the boomer, buster, or builder generations. It also works with its own unique church culture. Finally, the church works with the local culture. Whether it's a Lutheran culture of Minnesota, a Southern Baptist culture of Atlanta, or an ungodly pagan culture of San Francisco, every church has its own local culture.

I'm convinced understanding your local culture is more important than knowing about your national culture. I'm working in northern California, which includes churches in Marin County, Napa County, Vallejo, and churches down in the San Joaquin Valley. Those local cultures are as different as night and day. What attracts some people in one culture turns off other people in a different culture. I find that most pastors and churches have no understanding of the local culture in which they live.

In terms of exegeting culture, how does this impact the way you go about preaching a sermon?

I tell stories of how we're going to touch our world; specifically the world in which the church finds itself. I want to make clear that what we may be doing here in Minneapolis is only going to work in Minneapolis, and here's why. You can walk up to an atheist on the street in Minneapolis and ask, "What religion are you?" and they're going to tell you, "Lutheran," because it's almost an ethnic thing. That's one of the reasons we're going to have a traditional service.

Suppose you carry this over to communicating vision in Minneapolis. While preaching about worship and music, I'd remind people that we're doing a traditional service not because people here like to sing the old hymns, but because we want to reach unchurched Lutherans. This is reminiscent of Paul saying, "When I'm with the Jews, I'm like a Jew," and, "When I'm with the Lutherans, I'm like a Lutheran."

I want people to know that whether it's the issue of worship, music, the way we do outreach, or why we're communicating the vision we do, it's determined not only by boomers, busters, and builders, but also by local cultural issues.

Okay, explore the same question relating to reaching out.

The biggest difference between growing churches and dying ones is . . . for whom they exist. Dying and plateaued churches exist for the people who are already there. Growing churches exist for people who aren't there yet. Within this latter group, the values of the church are consistent with the mission and the vision. The church is also structured to fulfill the mission and the vision. Many churches have never thought through the fact that their structure may be hindering their very mission, even though they might have the supporting values.

As I am preaching about change, the direction we want to go, and why the staff is making decisions that were previously made by committees and boards, I want them to understand that we are making every possible decision in the church for the benefit of people who aren't here yet.

Therefore, if we're going to do a traditional service, we do it because we're in the type of community where unbelievers will be attracted by this type of service, not because we have a number of older people who like that style. If we're going to do a contemporary service, we're going to build one that meets our local cultural needs, which might be calling for a less traditional service devoid of hymns and liturgy.

Will you summarize how this relates primarily to the week-to-week preparation of a sermon on reaching out?

When I'm preparing my sermon, I've got to figure out how to communicate biblical and theological concepts in the language of people who are either unchurched, dechurched, or believers coming with very limited knowledge of the Bible. I never use "the Greek says." We never talk about terms like *propitiation* and *transubstantiation.* If I want to talk about the federal headship of Adam, I talk about the fact that God created a world much like our government where there was a representative, and Adam got to be my hero. I talk about the federal headship of Adam in a way that will communicate to people who have little biblical background.

So as a preacher, I not only think through what I'm going to say, but also how I'm going to say it, particularly in this new paradigm as a leader.

How would you respond to those who might hear this and react: Is he saying we should stop preaching the Bible or stop expository preaching of the Scriptures?

I would say two things. First, if I'm going to go topical, I'd better be able to sit down and develop a biblical theology. My big idea must be rooted in exegesis. It has to be anchored with integrity in the text, though it may not come out of one text.

Second, I must do more than simply handle a text with integrity. I must also think about application and how I fulfill my role as a leader. That means I tell stories. It means I'm positive. It means I'm asking the "so what?" question of the community. This helps the church to understand that the vital areas of worship, teaching, fellowship, and evangelism are things we do together, not simply as individuals.

I hear you saying that however you preach, whether it's expository or topical, you can preach as a leader if you're focusing on a kind of leadership grid as you prepare. It's as if there are five or six things you're always checking off when it comes to application.

That's correct. Preaching as a leader is challenging but doable if you prepare with these key demands in mind. Prepare with vision, recruitment, and resource procurement integrated into your planning. Know your local church culture. Preach to the community rather than the individual. Remember to keep it positive. These are key tasks if you want to preach as a leader.

Paul Borden is executive minister of Growing Healthy Churches and author of *Hit the Bullseye* and *Assaulting the Gates.*